Straightforward

Intermediate **Workbook**

with answer key

MACMILLAN

Macmillan Education
Between Towns Road, Oxford OX4 3PP
A division of Macmillan Publishers Limited

Companies and representatives throughout the world

ISBN 978-0-230-42328-2 Workbook
ISBN 978-0-230-42327-5 Workbook plus Answer Key
ISBN 978-0-230-42326-8 Workbook plus Answer Key and Workbook Audio CD
ISBN 978-0-230-42325-1 Workbook and Workbook Audio CD

Designed by eMC Design Ltd.
Illustrated by Paul Daviz, Darren Lingrad, Peter Lubach, Mark Ruffle, Martin Shovel.
Macmillan Reader Illustrations © Macmillan Publishers Limited 2002, 2005
Cover design by eMC Design Ltd.
Cover photograph by Corbis/L.E.Frank (main); Alamy/Robert Harding Picture Library, Alamy/Images & Stories; Corbis/G.Kalt; Corbis/R.Tidman; Getty/D.Chinnery.
Picture research by Suzanne Williams

Author's acknowledgements
I would like to thank Janet Castro and Nicola Stewart for their support on this project.

The publishers would like to thank all the teachers from around the world who provided invaluable comments, suggestions and feedback on the first edition. The publishers would also like to thank Mike Sayer and the following people for their help and contribution to the second edition:
Tatiana Baytimerova (Russia), Lenka Boehmová (Czech Republic), Dr. Manuel Padilla Cruz (Spain), Svetlana Elchaninova (Russia), Jennifer Díaz Green (Dublin), Elena Mokeeva (Romania), Lynn Thomson (freelance editor), Amany Shawkey (Macmillan Egypt), Maria Teresa Rius Villaplana (Spain), Natalia Vorobyeva (Russia).

The author and publishers are grateful for permission to reprint the following copyright material:
Page 28: Statistical information from HMSO website www.statistics.gov.uk used with permission;
Page 44: Extracts from 'Food makers to market more healthy foods for kids' taken from website www.foodnavigator.com;
Page 90: Material from 'Meet me in Istanbul' by Richard Chisholm, copyright © Richard Chisholm, first published 1979 for Macmillan Readers, reprinted by permission of the publisher.

The authors and publishers would like to thank the following for permission to reproduce their photographs:
Alamy/67photo p15, Alamy/Jon Arnold Images Ltd p66, Alamy/BL Images Ltd p50, Alamy/Richard Cooke p31, Alamy/David Fleetham p75(b), Alamy/Gavin Hellier/Robert Harding World Picture Library Ltd p31, Alamy/Juice Images p8, Alamy/Art Kowalsky p30, Alamy/Tom Merton p36, Alamy/Mirrorpix/Trinity Mirror p53, Alamy/Laurence Mouton/ PhotoAlto p68, Alamy/Chris Rout p7(tl), Alamy/Stella/Imagebroker p30, Alamy/Vstock p54, Alamy/Westmacott p84, Alamy/Gerry Yardy p6(tl); **Bananastock** p69(cr,cl); **Corbis**/Ron Dahlquist/ Terra p75(t), Corbis/Kurt Hutton/Hulton-Deutsch Collection p16, Corbis/Colin McPherson/Corbis Sports p58, Corbis/Ris Images/Ivy p87, Digital Stock/Corbis p69(c,br); **Getty Images** p69(bl), Getty Images/Able Images/Photodisc p73, Getty Images/BLOOM Image p28, Getty Images/Buena Vista Images/The Image Bank p74, Getty Images/Elea Dumas/Foodpix p44, Getty Images/Grant Faint/ The Image Bank p69(t), Getty Images/Ghislain & Marie David de Lossy/The Image Bank p35, Getty Images/Bruno DeHogues/Photographers Choice p11, Getty Images/Robert Harding/Digital Vision p72, Getty Images/Tim Hawley/ Photographer's Choice p24(c), Getty Images/Martin Harvey/Gallo Images p10, Getty Images/Bruce Hershey/Workbook Stock p18, Getty Images/Alberto Incrocci/Stone p39, Getty/Latitudestock/Gallo Images p6(cl), Getty Images/Davis McGlynn/Photographer's Choice p21, Getty Images/Thomas Northcut/Photodisc p24(t), Getty Images/Charriau Pierre/Photographer's Choice p23, Getty Images/ Mark Scott/Taxi p56(baseball), Getty Images/Stockbyte p56(tennis), Getty Images/Tom Till/Photographer's Choice p51, Getty Images/Mitch Tobias/ Photographer's Choice p38, Getty Images/Jim Watson p49; **PA Photos**/Steve Coleman/AP p63, PA Photos/Hayden West/PA Archive p70; **Photolibrary**/ Aurore, Belkin/ArabianEye p48, Photolibrary/David Harrigan/Ableimages p7(tml), Photolibrary/Grant Prichard/Britain on View p84, Photolibrary/Ariel Skelley/Flirt Collection p45; **Rex Features**/Geoff Pugh p13, Rex Features/Mike Webster p9.

These materials may contain links for third party websites. We have no control over, and are not responsible for, the contents of such third party websites. Please use care when accessing them.

Although we have tried to trace and contact copyright holders before publication, in some cases this has not been possible. If contacted we will be pleased to rectify any errors or omissions at the earliest opportunity.

Printed and bound in Thailand

2016 2015 2014 2013
10 9 8 7 6 5 4 3

Contents

p4	1A–1D	Stative & dynamic verbs; Present simple & present continuous; Verbs with two meanings; Subject & object questions; Self-image; Describing people
p8	1 Reading	*You never get a second chance to make a first impression*
p9	2A–2D	Present perfect & past simple; Present perfect for unfinished time; Phrasal verbs; Travelling; Verb collocations (travel)
p13	2 Reading	*Eddie Izzard – the marathon man!*
p14	3A–3D	Modals of obligation, permission & prohibition (present time); *Make, let & allow*; Modals of obligation, permission & prohibition (past time); Accommodation; Verb collocations (sleep); Requests
p18	3 Reading	*Interview*
p19	4A–4D	Past simple & past continuous; *Both & neither*; Past perfect simple; Talking about similarities & differences; Injuries; Time linkers
p23	4 Reading	*A win on the horses*
p24	5A–5D	Comparisions 1; Comparisions 2; Comparing nouns; Adjectives (advertising); Adjectives (negative prefixes); Office activities; Office supplies; On the phone
p28	5 Reading	*Statistics*
p29	6A–6D	Future 1 (future plans); Future 2 (predictions); Present tenses in future time clauses; Indirect questions; Holidays 1; Holidays 2; Collocations with *sound*
p33	6 Reading	*What is the real price of tourism?*
p34	7A–7D	Present perfect continuous 1; Present perfect continuous 2; Phrasal verbs with *live*; Metaphor; Life stages; Giving advice; Exclamations with *What*
p38	7 Reading	*Downshifting – a way of living*
p39	8A–8D	*Would*; Unreal conditions (type 2); Unreal conditions (type 3); Newspapers; Offers; Compound nouns (driving); Law & order
p43	8 Reading	*The future of the press?*
p44	9A–9D	Articles & determiners; Quantifiers 1; Quantifiers 2; Prepositional phrases; Containers; Shopping; Collocations with *take*; Complaints
p48	9 Reading	*The world's greatest shopping malls*
p49	10A–10D	Modals of speculation 1 (present time); Modals of speculation 2 (present time); Modals of speculation (past time); Verbs followed by infinitive; Illusions; Word families; Advantages & disadvantages; Idioms
p53	10 Reading	*'Lucky' Lord Lucan – alive or dead?*
p54	11A–11D	Passive; Verbs with two objects; Causative; *Make & do*; Question tags (checking); Sport; Nouns & adjectives (describing people); Services
p58	11 Reading	*Britain's most unusual sporting event*
p59	12A–12D	Reported speech & thought; Reported questions; *Tell & ask* with infinitive; Reporting verbs; Verb collocations (money); Social expressions
p63	12 Reading	*Oseola McCarty*

Writing

p64	1	A description of a best friend
p66	2	A description of a town or city
p68	3	Advantages and disadvantages
p70	4	A narrative: lottery winner
p72	5	An advertisement
p74	6	An extract from a holiday brochure
p76	7	A letter of advice
p78	8	A funny crime story
p80	9	A letter of complaint
p82	10	A narrative
p84	11	A description of a sporting event
p86	12	Writing a report

Useful language to improve your writing p88   **Irregular verbs** p89
Extract from *Meet me in Istanbul* **by Richard Chisholm** p90   **Answer key** pi

1A Double lives

Stative & dynamic verbs

1 Choose the correct verb form to complete the sentences.

1 You're lying! I *don't believe / 'm not believing* what you're saying.
2 Clara *thinks / is thinking* of changing her job.
3 I *want / am wanting* to watch *Mad Men* on TV.
4 She says that she *likes / is liking* me, but I'm not sure.
5 This day out at the funfair *costs / is costing* me a fortune.
6 I *hate / am hating* people who lie.

2 Find and correct six grammatical mistakes in the verbs in the advertisement.

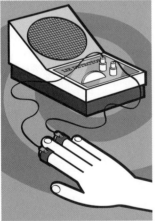

Are you believing your partner when they say they're working late at the office?

How are you knowing if he or she is telling the truth?

Easy!

▸ Buy the person you are loving the Lie Detector.
▸ This unique device can tell if a person is lying or not.
▸ It is asking a simple question. If the person is lying, they get an electric shock. If they are telling the truth, nothing happens.

It couldn't be easier.

So if you think about what you are wanting to buy your loved one, think no more – **Trickster Toys** has the perfect gift for him or her.

Every couple should have one.

Vocabulary from the lesson

3 Underline the word or phrase that does not go with the verb.

1 **lie** about why you're late   to a friend   about your age   by a member of your family
2 **have** no choice   a lovely time   sincere   no qualifications
3 **look** ahead someone   up to someone   great   at someone straight in the eyes
4 **be** dating someone   fidgeting and nervous   honesty   a liar
5 **tell** the truth   about a story   a lie   your partner something

4 Complete the dialogue with words from the box.

fidgeting	sweaty	liar	date	great	nervous

Meena: You look fantastic, Gabrielle.
Gabrielle: Oh, you (1) _____!
Meena: I'm not lying! You look (2) _____.
Gabrielle: But I'm feeling really (3) _____.
Meena: Relax. What can go wrong?
Gabrielle: On a first (4) _____!? Plenty!
Meena: He's probably going to feel uncomfortable, too.
Gabrielle: Not as much as me. My hands are all (5) _____.
Meena: It would help if you could stop (6) _____ with your hair.

🔊 Dictation

5 🔊 01 Write the sentences that you hear.

1 _____?
2 _____.
3 _____.
4 _____.
5 _____.
6 _____.

💿 Read & listen

6 💿 02 Read and listen to the reading text *Liars!* on page 6 of the Student's Book.

1B | Daily lives

PRESENT SIMPLE & PRESENT CONTINUOUS

1 Choose the correct verb forms to complete the interview.

I: Tonight I (1) *interview / am interviewing* the world famous model, Tania Brookes. Tania, welcome.

T: Thanks, James.

I: Now I'd like to start by asking you about this new reality TV programme you (2) *do / are doing* called *Swapping Jobs*.

T: Yep. Basically, I swap jobs for a week with someone … with Dot Bryce, in fact. Dot is a single working parent with three kids. She (3) *lives / is living* in a small flat and (4) *works / is working* as a cleaning lady.

I: And how does her life compare to yours?

T: To be honest, there's no comparison. Let me give you an example. In a normal photo shoot I (5) *make / am making* about £300 per hour. That is 50 times more than Dot makes in the same time!

I: Wow! Do you feel sorry for her?

T: Not at all. She's a terrific woman: strong, optimistic and fun. We actually (6) *like / are liking* each other a lot. And she (7) *has / is having* three lovely girls.

I: OK, tell us a little about your new job.

T: OK. I (8) *get / am getting* up at six and take the girls to school for 8.30. Then it's a bus ride to my first job. I seem to spend a lot of time on buses! Anyway, the work is non-stop. At the moment I (9) *do / am doing* stuff like washing dishes, cleaning floors, baths and toilets, hoovering carpets, tidying up rooms, and so on.

I: And (10) *do you enjoy / are you enjoying* it?

T: Is that a serious question!? No way!

VERBS WITH TWO MEANINGS

2 Complete the dialogue. Put the verbs in brackets into the present simple or present continuous.

Alan: I (1) _____ (*think*) about going on that *Swapping Jobs* programme.

Bob: I (2) _____ (*not / think*) they'll want you.

Alan: Why not? I (3) _____ (*have*) an interesting job.

Bob: Alan, forget it! You're a traffic warden. That is not an interesting job!

Alan: Well, you're wrong. Look at this. A letter from AVD TV.

Bob: What!?

Alan: Yep! I (4) _____ (*see*) them for a meeting tomorrow. Being a traffic warden is one of the most unpopular jobs in Britain, you know.

Bob: Yeah, I know. So?

Alan: Well, that means a lot of people would love to see someone famous doing my job.

Bob: Oh, I (5) _____ (*see*) what you mean. So the idea is to watch someone who (6) _____ (*have*) a really bad time for a week.

Alan: That's the idea.

Bob: I don't believe it!

TRANSLATION

3 Translate the sentences into your language.

1 I normally vote for the Liberal Democrats in general elections.

   _____.

2 What are you doing at the moment?

   _____?

3 She's trying to explain, but he doesn't seem to understand her.

   _____.

4 I'm thinking of going to Poland on holiday this summer.

   _____.

5 I'm working in a bar until I can find a better job.

   _____.

6 I think reality TV is usually complete rubbish.

   _____.

1c | Britishness

SUBJECT & OBJECT QUESTIONS

1 How much do you know about Britain today? Do the quiz to find out.

DO YOU KNOW ...

1 **Which countries form Britain?**
   a) England and Scotland
   b) England, Scotland and Wales
   c) England, Scotland, Wales and Northern Ireland

2 **What does Cymru mean?**
   a) It's Welsh for 'Good morning'.
   b) It's Welsh for 'Goodbye'. c) It's Welsh for 'Wales'.

3 **Where did Shakespeare live?**
   a) in Manchester
   b) in Stratford upon Avon c) in York

4 **What is the most popular restaurant dish in Britain?**
   a) a curry dish called Chicken Tikka Masala
   b) roast beef c) fish and chips

5 **What famous building does the Queen officially open every year with a speech?**
   a) Parliament b) Buckingham Palace
   c) The White House

6 **What ancient language do some people in Scotland speak?**
   a) Gaelic b) Celtic c) Basque

Which of the questions are subject questions (S) and which are object questions (O)?

2 Choose the correct verb form to complete the questions.

1 Who *did write / wrote* Hamlet?
2 How many countries *do belong / belong* to the European Union?
3 What does BBC *stand / stands* for?
4 How many people *do live / live* in Britain?
5 Who *did win / won* the general election in 2010?
6 What percentage of seats in parliament do *women hold / hold women*?

3 Match the answers a–f to the questions 1–6 in exercise 2.

- [ ] a the British Broadcasting Corporation
- [ ] b the Conservatives and Liberal Democrats
- [ ] c There are 27 member states.
- [ ] d 20%
- [ ] e 60 million
- [ ] f Shakespeare

4 Write a question for every answer.

1 What _____?
  Spiders and horror films frighten me.

2 Who _____?
  My favourite British writer is Charles Dickens.

3 Where _____?
  I live in Cardiff, the capital of Wales.

4 Which party _____?
  I voted for the Green Party.

SELF-IMAGE

5 Complete the sentences in column A with a phrase from column B.

A	B
1 I consider myself lucky to have a job	a first and as British second.
2 My children probably see	b but I love playing tennis.
3 I think of myself as a European	c because there is very little work around.
4 I would describe myself	d friend I have.
5 I don't see myself as a great player,	e me as an old dinosaur.
6 I'm proud to be British because	f of our long history.
7 My wife is the best	g as open and friendly.

DICTATION

6 03 Write the sentences that you hear.

1 _____.

2 _____.

3 _____?

4 _____?

5 _____.

6 _____?

1D First impressions

DESCRIBING PEOPLE

1 Complete the dialogue between two friends, Jake and Anita, with words or phrases from the box.

> eyes   shaved   What does he look like
> pale   prominent   blond
> muscular   straight   what's his hair like

J: My new flatmate moved in today. His name's Neil.

A: Oh, right. (1) _____?

J: Well, he's tall and he's got a (2) _____ build. I think he goes to the gym a lot. And he's got a (3) _____ complexion.

A: So, he's really sporty?

J: Yeah.

A: Well, that's good. You like sport, too. Anything else? Does he have a really big, (4) _____ nose?

J: No, nothing like that. He's got a very ordinary, (5) _____ nose.

A: And (6) _____? Is he completely bald?

J: Well, actually, his hair is really short. He's got a (7) _____ head.

A: Oh, right.

J: Yes, and his hair's (8) _____. And he's got big, blue (9) _____.

A: Oh, right. Is he Swedish?

J: No, but I know what you mean.

A: OK. Well, he sounds OK. Hope you two get on together in the flat.

2 Read the dialogue again. Which picture shows Neil, A or B?

3 Underline the word that does not go with the noun.

1 **complexion**	pale	shaved	tanned
2 **build**	wide	muscular	average
3 **head**	bald	round	healthy
4 **eyes**	dark	blond	narrow
5 **hair**	wavy	prominent	shiny
6 **nose**	slim	pointed	prominent

4 Choose the correct phrase to complete the sentences.

1 Does she look *as if / like* her mother?
2 They look *as if / like* boyfriend and girlfriend.
3 My mother *looks like / looks* very tired. I think she works too much.
4 Are you OK? You *look as if / look* you have just seen a ghost.
5 He *looks like / looks* that film star, Orlando Bloom.
6 She *looks like / looks* French. I think it's because of her clothes.

TRANSLATION

5 Translate the sentences into your language.

1 What's your new flatmate like?

_____?

2 He looks as if he has had some very bad news.

_____.

3 What does his brother look like?

_____?

4 He's bald, quite muscular and tanned, and has got big green eyes.

_____

_____.

5 She's average build and has got dark brown hair and eyes, and a prominent nose.

_____

_____.

1 | Reading

You never get a
second chance
to make a first impression

When two people meet for the first time, physical impressions are immediate. Before they have a chance to say a word, their senses are in overdrive; they are picking up and storing information about each other.
5 They register looks, smell and body language. They use eye contact to support the process and to establish a relationship. Within a few seconds, they have made a mental picture of each other. On the basis of this tiny amount of data, they form opinions which they use in the future.

10 But just how reliable are first impressions? Take the story of Jake and Caroline. Jake didn't like Caroline when he first met her. 'She seemed cold and distant. She made almost no eye contact and she didn't seem to listen to me.' Six months later, they met again. 'Caroline was a completely different person.
15 She was warm, friendly and smiled a lot. When she told me that her father had died two days before we first met, that explained everything. It taught me to be more careful about making assumptions about people based on first impressions.'

However wrong they can be, first impressions are a necessary
20 survival mechanism. Thousands of years ago they helped people decide how to react in potentially dangerous situations. That is still true today, although in most cases it is not a question of life and death. According to some, we can learn to read first impressions better. We can also learn to create more
25 powerful first impressions. Professor Helen Trent, a specialist in interpersonal relations, has studied the practice of good communicators. 'Research shows that people who can make others feel good about themselves are excellent at creating positive first impressions. We call these people 'Powerful
30 Communicators' or PCs. You can tell when you meet one; you feel really good afterwards and you think "What a nice person." PCs immediately get in sync with the other person; they coordinate their body language and smiles with their partner. They also maintain eye contact and sound and look as
35 if they are interested, although sometimes they are not. These actions make the other person feel good about the experience.' PCs are winners in the first-impressions race. So if you want to be a PC, start training and remember, you only get one chance to make a great first impression!

---

1 Read the article. Complete the sentences 1–5 with the best answers a–c.

1 The moment two people first meet they …
   a) look at and talk to each other.   b) look at each other.
   c) look at each other and build a picture of each other.
2 The story about Jake and Caroline shows that …
   a) problems stop communication.
   b) we can make mistakes based on first impressions.
   c) they liked each other in the end.
3 Studying good communicators tells us that they…
   a) make us feel positive.
   b) make us feel friendly.
   c) make us feel like good communicators, too.
4 Powerful communicators …   a) do not always know the effect they have on the other person.
   b) are never honest.   c) are not always honest.
5 PCs are …   a) the best at running.
   b) the best at winning.
   c) the best at creating positive first impressions.

2 Match the words and phrases 1–6 to the definitions a–f. The line numbers are in brackets.

1 are in overdrive (3)   4 get in sync (32)
2 data (8)   5 survival mechanism (20)
3 reliable (10)   6 assumptions (18)

☐ a make two or more things happen at the same time
☐ b something that helps you stay alive
☐ c be very active or too active
☐ d information
☐ e something (or someone) that you can depend on
☐ f things that you think are true, but you cannot be certain

🔊 READ & LISTEN

3 🔊 **04** Listen to Reading 1 *You never get a second chance to make a first impression* on the CD and read the article again.

2A | Around the world

Vocabulary from the lesson

1 Complete the sentences with words from the box.

travels	trip	travel
adventure	journey	hitchhiked

1 We haven't finished planning our _____ to Croatia yet, but we're going for two weeks.

2 My aunt made lots of trips to India and now she is writing a book about her _____ there.

3 My hobbies are sports and _____. Last year I went on a two-month trip around South America.

4 Travelling around Indonesia was an incredible _____ – we saw some amazing things and met some wonderful people.

5 I've _____ all over Europe. The best lift I ever had was from France to Hungary.

6 The _____ from Turkey to India was long and difficult.

Present perfect & past simple

2 Find and correct six mistakes in the review.

I've just finished *Long Way Round*, a book about an incredible around-the-world journey written by two British actors, Ewan McGregor and Charley Boorman. The story has started one day when McGregor was looking at a map of the world. He has realized that it was possible to ride all the way around the world by motorbike. He suggested the idea over dinner to his good friend, Boorman. Boorman has immediately agreed. The result, 20,000 miles and three months later, is a very entertaining travel book that I didn't want to put down. On the journey they have experienced terrible weather and road conditions and they have had all sorts of adventures, including a meeting with Mongolian nomads and gun-carrying Ukrainians. *Long Way Round* is action-packed and was a real success for the two actors.

3 Complete the dialogue between a mother (M) and her daughter (D). Put the verbs in brackets into the present perfect or past simple.

D: Hi, Mum! I (1) _____ just _____ (*get back*).

M: Oh, Amy, welcome home, darling! When (2) _____ you _____ (*get back*)?

D: Yesterday! The plane (3) _____ (*land*) at about 10pm.

M: Oh, I was so worried. The last time I (4) _____ (*have*) any news was that call from Tanzania. Where (5) _____ you _____ (*be*) since then?

D: Oh, everywhere. We (6) _____ (*go*) to Uganda, Malawi and Mozambique.

M: 'We'? Who's 'we'?

D: Oh, mum. I (7) _____ (*meet*) a fantastic man. His name is Brian.

M: That's wonderful, dear. Where (8) _____ you _____ (*meet*)?

D: On a safari in Kenya. And I've got some great news for you and dad. We (9) _____ (*get married*).

M: Married! When (10) _____ you _____ (*get married*)?

D: I'll tell you all about it when we see you tonight. Brian and I want to take you out for dinner.

🔊 Dictation

4 🔊 **05** Write the sentences that you hear.

1 _____ .

2 _____ .

3 _____ ?

4 _____ .

5 _____ .

6 _____ .

🔊 Read & listen

5 🔊 **06** Read and listen to the reading text *Lawyer gives up job to cycle around the world* on page 16 of the Student's Book.

2B | Unusual journeys

Phrasal verbs

1 The particles underlined are in the wrong sentences. Rearrange the particles to make the sentences correct.

1 We couldn't go to Brazil because we didn't have enough time to sort the visas <u>up</u>.
2 I came <u>off</u> this old lamp in a Moroccan market.
3 The medicine helped me get <u>off</u> the malaria.
4 After two days in the truck the driver dropped me <u>out</u>.
5 I waited for eight hours and eventually a car picked me <u>over</u>.
6 All my friends saw me <u>across</u> at the airport.

2 Complete the email with phrasal verbs from exercise 1 in the correct form.

○○○

⁞ File   Edit   View   Favourites   Tools   Help   Links ➤

Hi Mum and Dad,

Well, I've finally made it to New Zealand. I can't believe that it's eighteen months since you (1) _____ me _____ at the airport. But this is definitely the last leg of my journey because I've spent almost all my money. When I was in Vietnam, I (2) _____ a wonderful, antique vase in a market and I just had to buy it. It was quite expensive, so that's why I'm broke.

Anyway, I've been hitchhiking here in New Zealand. A lorry driver (3) _____ me _____ in Wellington and (4) _____ me _____ by the coast in the south of the country. So, that was really lucky. I've found a nice hostel to stay in and I've met two travellers from England and we're hanging out together. They've been quite unlucky on their trip. One of them had a problem with his passport, but, fortunately, he (5) _____ it _____ now. And the other had malaria. Fortunately, he (6) _____ it now. He's looking healthy again.

I'm flying home on Sunday.

Looking forward to seeing you.

Love,
Matthew xx

---

3 The particles in the sentences are in the wrong place. Put them in the correct place.

1 Did you get your illness over in a hospital?
2 The villagers offered to look my motorbike after.
3 Could you drop off us in Paris, please?
4 I came an old school friend in a tea house across in Darjeeling, India.
5 We sorted a lift to La Paz in Bolivia out.
6 The doctor's family looked me after when I got malaria in Pakistan.

Translation

4 Translate the dialogue into your language.

Andrew: Have you ever hitchhiked anywhere?
Darina: Yes, lots of places when I was younger.
Andrew: And where did you go?
Darina: Oh, I travelled around Europe and I went to America in 1992. And how about you? Have you ever hitchhiked?
Andrew: No, never. I've never liked the idea of hitchhiking. Did you ever have any problems on your trips?
Darina: Yes, once. When I was in Nebraska I waited for eight hours in the snow until someone stopped and gave me a lift.
Andrew: Really!?
Darina: Yeah. I've never been so cold in my whole life!

2c | Down under

PRESENT PERFECT FOR UNFINISHED TIME

1 Complete the phone dialogue between Pia (P) and Jenny (J) with the correct form of the verbs in brackets.

P: Hello? Jenny?

J: Pia? I thought you were in Greece.

P: We are. We (1) _____ (*get*) here five days ago.

J: Yes, you left on Saturday, didn't you? Are you enjoying the sailing?

P: Oh, yes. Absolutely amazing! We (2) _____ (*visit*) three islands in the last three days. And last night we (3) _____ (*have*) dinner on the beach. It was so romantic.

J: Lovely! And how's the weather?

P: It (4) _____ (*be*) very hot. It (5) _____ (*be*) so hot last night that we slept outside on the deck of the boat. I (6) _____ (*never / see*) so many stars.

J: Oh, that sounds beautiful.

P: Yes, very. Anyway, could you do me a favour, Jenny?

J: Sure. If I can.

P: I think I (7) _____ (*leave*) the back door open when we left the house.

J: Oh, dear. I've got your keys. I'll pop over and check.

P: Oh, thank you. I (8) _____ (*be*) so worried.

J: Well, stop worrying now. Just have a lovely time.

P: We will. Thanks again.

2 Choose the correct time expression to complete the sentences.

1 They flew to Tokyo *last week / over the last week*.
2 We've met some nice people *two weeks ago / during the last two weeks*.
3 I haven't been to Australia *last year / up till now*.
4 My sister has visited eight different countries *over the last two months / last month*.
5 They haven't been abroad *in 1990 / since 1990*.
6 Have you read any good travel books *recently / last summer*?

VOCABULARY FROM THE LESSON

3 Complete the travel guide with phrases from the box.

> settle down   best-known monuments
> cultural and historical   popular destination
> landmark   so many things to see and do

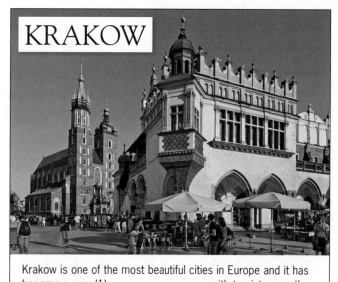

KRAKOW

Krakow is one of the most beautiful cities in Europe and it has become a very (1) _____ with tourists over the last few years. Whether you are looking for history or for an amazing night on the town, there are (2) _____ here.

The city has a long (3) _____ tradition and was the capital of Poland for six centuries. It's a small city and easy to get around. Follow the 'Route of the Saints', a trip which will take you to sixteen of the 72 churches for which Krakow is so famous. Take a horse and cart up Wawel Hill to see two of Krakow's (4) _____: the cathedral and the Royal Castle. You should also visit the Jagiellonian University, which is one of the oldest in Europe.

Don't miss out on the other things this wonderful city has to offer; the shopping is good and the nightlife is excellent. Finally, whatever you do, visit the Rynek Glowny, that other famous Krakowian (5) _____. It is the largest medieval square in Europe and the focus of much of Krakow's social life. So pull up a chair in one of the restaurants, bars or cafés, (6) _____ and watch the world go by.

🔊 DICTATION

4 🔊 **07** Write the dialogue that you hear.

_____

_____

_____

_____

_____

_____

_____

_____

_____

2D | Getting around

TRAVELLING

1 Rearrange the words to make sentences.

1 airport , please to the a single .

_____

2 tell me , please the time of the next train could you to Bristol ?

_____

3 a five-pound note have you change for got , please ?

_____

4 we get to , please tell me when York Road could you ?

_____

5 a cab for Dorset Road I'd like , please in Ealing .

_____

6 get a taxi around here anywhere can I ?

_____

2 Imagine that you are studying English in a language school in London. Take this quiz in a school magazine and see how many questions you can answer.

How well could you survive on public transport in London?

1 You are at the train station and need to know what time the next train to Plymouth leaves. What do you say?

_____

2 You are in your hotel room and want a cab to go to Piccadilly Circus in London. What do you say to the receptionist?

_____

3 You get on a bus and you only have a five-pound note. What do you say to the driver?

_____

4 You are at the train station and you want a first-class return ticket to Manchester. What do you say?

_____

5 You are in the street and need to catch a taxi. You stop a person and ask for a taxi rank. What do you say?

_____

6 You are on a bus, but you don't know where the stop for Church Road is. What do you say to the person next to you?

_____

VERB COLLOCATIONS (TRAVEL)

3 Complete the story with verbs from the box.

get off	missed
arrived	take
drop	walk
catch	took

I flew to Paris once for an important business meeting and when I landed, I decided to (1) _____ the bus into town. I thought I had lots of time. Unfortunately, I (2) _____ the bus and had to wait twenty minutes for the next one. When it came, I got on, but the traffic was terrible. So I decided to (3) _____ and I (4) _____ a taxi instead. I asked the driver to take me straight to the meeting. After 40 minutes in the taxi, it was clear I was going to be late. I asked the driver to (5) _____ me off by the Pont Neuf, a bridge by the river Seine. I wanted to (6) _____ to the meeting because of the terrible traffic. I thought it would (7) _____ about 20 minutes, but I was wrong. The streets were full of people and I was carrying two heavy bags. I finally (8) _____ at the building an hour later and it was shut. Then I realized it was May 1 and a public holiday in France! The meeting wasn't until the next day! What an idiot!!

TRANSLATION

4 Translate the sentences into your language.

1 There are special tickets that allow you to get on and off the tour bus when you want.

_____.

2 Excuse me. Have I missed the 12.08 to Liverpool?

_____?

3 Could you tell me the time of the next train to Glasgow, please?

_____?

4 I'd like a cab for the Royal Plaza Hotel, please.

_____.

5 Did you get a single or a return ticket to Berlin?

_____?

2 | Reading

1 Read the article about Eddie Izzard. Tick the five achievements in the list below which, according to the article, Eddie has achieved.

☐ 1 He has performed his comedy show all over Europe.
☐ 2 He has been in well-known American films.
☐ 3 He has run over 40 marathons.
☐ 4 He has appeared in British TV series.
☐ 5 He has run a leading charity.

☐ 6 He has completed a marathon in Wales.
☐ 7 He has appeared in London theatres.
☐ 8 He has finished a triathlon.
☐ 9 He has won the London Marathon.

EDDIE IZZARD – THE MARATHON MAN!

Eddie Izzard is well known in the English-speaking world as a funny and talented comedian. He has performed his live comedy show to huge audiences and he has also appeared in a number of
5 successful Hollywood films, including *Ocean's Twelve* and *Ocean's Thirteen*. He has played leading theatrical roles on London's West End and New York's Broadway, and he has even been in an American TV series, although he has never made a TV series for British TV. However, he has
10 also achieved something quite incredible that nobody ever expected him to do – he has run 43 marathons in 51 days!

In 2009, Eddie decided he wanted to do something to raise money for Comic Relief, a popular charity which a lot of famous comedians support. He had only five weeks
15 of training before he set out on his epic run around Britain, and when he ran the first marathon he found it really tough. It took him almost ten hours to complete the course, which is very slow. However, he got faster and faster as he continued to run marathons. Soon, he was
20 running marathons in under five hours – which is not bad, especially as Eddie had never been a serious runner before!

Eddie started his marathon adventure in London in late July 2009 and headed west towards Cardiff. His plan was
25 to run in England, Wales, Northern Ireland and Scotland, and to visit the capital cities of all four countries. He managed to do this – he also carried the flag of each country when he was running there! When he finished his last marathon, crossing the finishing line in Trafalgar
30 Square in London, he had been running a marathon a day, six days a week for seven weeks. He ran over 1,700 kilometres!

Since running the marathons, Eddie has become more interested in keeping fit. He has competed in the
35 Ironman triathlon and in other charity events, and he has pointed out that once you are really fit, it's a good idea to stay that way!

2 Read the article again and decide if the sentences are true (T) or false (F). Correct the false sentences.

1 Eddie usually performs in small theatres. ___
2 Eddie has only made two Hollywood films. ___
3 Eddie ran the marathons for charity. ___
4 Eddie spent months training to be ready to run the marathons. ___
5 It took him less time to run the last marathon than the first. ___
6 Eddie didn't run any marathons in Scotland. ___
7 Eddie has decided never to do any more tough endurance events. ___

3 Find words or phrases in the text that match the definitions 1–6. The paragraph numbers are in brackets.

1 very good at what he does (1)
2 very big (1)
3 difficult (2)
4 fairly good (3)
5 went in the direction of (3)
6 explained (4)

🔘 READ & LISTEN

4 🔘 **08** Listen to Reading 2 *Eddie Izzard – the marathon man!* on the CD and read the article again.

3A | Dream homes

MODALS OF OBLIGATION, PERMISSION & PROHIBITION (PRESENT TIME)

1 Four people are looking for somewhere to live. Read the two adverts and then read what the four people are looking for. Match the adverts 1–2 to the people a–d.

Advert 1

Looking for third person to share three-bedroom flat.

Rent £460 per calendar month for double room. Well-equipped: microwave, washer dryer, dishwasher, widescreen TV, etc. Very near tube and buses.

You don't need to pay any extra bills apart from phone, as all bills included in rent. Tenants are allowed to smoke in the flat. Please note that we can't accept pets because flat's too small.

Advert 2

Looking for fourth person to share large, quiet house with big garden.

Must be non-smoker and would prefer vegetarian.

£640 per month, including bills, for extra large double bedroom with view of garden. House not near public transport, but has off-street parking.

We have a cleaner, but you'll have to take care of your own room. Owner allows pets, providing they are small.

Please note that everyone has to turn down TV and music after 10pm as people have to get up early.

2 Choose the correct phrase to complete the sentences.

1 You *don't need to / can't* clean the house because we have a cleaner.

2 I'm sorry, but you *have to / aren't allowed to* smoke in the flat.

3 You *don't need to / are allowed to* pay a deposit.

4 I'm afraid that you *are allowed to / can't* park your car here.

5 You *can / don't need to* have visitors any time you like.

6 If you like, you *don't have to / can* park your car in the garage.

7 Your room has its own entrance, so you *are allowed to / don't have to* worry about disturbing others if you come home late at night.

8 You *can't / have to* pay your rent on the last day of the month at the latest.

Person a

I can afford up to £500 a month. I'd prefer a double, but I'm OK with a single room. It's really important that I'm near public transport as I haven't got a car. What else do I want?

Oh, I love cooking, so the kitchen should be well-equipped. I'm a smoker! I also love football, so my dream place would have one of those massive screens. That would be just perfect.

Person b

I have a pretty busy life, so what I'm looking for is a bit of peace and quiet. I absolutely hate housework, so ideally want somewhere where I have to do the minimum and I'm prepared to pay for that – up to £1,000 a month, not including bills. Would be ideal if there was somewhere I could park my car, too. Finally, I'm into sports and have a healthy lifestyle, so no smokers, please!

Person c

Money's not a problem at the moment. Much more important is a big room with light as I'm a painter. Ideally I'd like a place which isn't noisy as I need to be able to concentrate. The other essential thing is Chloe, my little dog. Whoever I share with has to be OK about pets. I'm a vegetarian and I don't smoke. Finally, I've got a motorbike, so transport links aren't that important.

Person d

I'm happy to pay up to £450 plus bills, but I do want a big room. My last flat had nowhere to wash clothes, so this place must have a washing machine at the very least.

Another thing – I don't have transport, so this place has to be close to good public transport. What else? Well, I'm a social smoker, so I'd prefer a place where I can have the occasional cigarette without people making me feel bad. Oh, and one final thing: I'm allergic to animals!

DICTATION

3 📀 **09** Write the sentences that you hear.

1 _____?

2 _____.

3 _____?

4 _____.

5 _____.

READ & LISTEN

4 📀 **10** Read and listen to the reading text *Paradise Ridge* on page 27 of the Student's Book.

3B | Unusual homes

VOCABULARY FROM THE LESSON

1 Complete the sentences with a word from the box.

> accommodation   share   facilities
> move   detached   local

1 In addition to the usual _____, the hotel also offers internet access and conference rooms.
2 She's going to move into a flat that belongs to the _____ authority.
3 There are three people living in the flat. They _____ the facilities and the bills.
4 There is not enough _____ for students in this town.
5 We're going to _____ house next year. We want to live somewhere bigger in the country.
6 This marvellous _____ house is surrounded by an enormous garden.

ACCOMMODATION

2 Complete the sentences with a word or phrase from the box.

> rented accommodation   terraced house
> holiday home   mobile home   suburbs
> apartment block   flat   tree house

1 My parents wanted to escape the English winters, so they bought a _____ in the south of Spain where they are going to live for four months a year.
2 We want to buy a house, but because we don't have enough money, we're living in _____.
3 Living in the _____ is so much quieter and greener than living in the town centre.
4 I live in a two-bedroom _____ on the third floor.
5 I hated living in an _____ because you had neighbours above and below you.
6 I like living in a _____ because you have neighbours on both sides of you.
7 The thing we love about our _____ is that we can drive wherever we want and always know we have our own beds to sleep in.
8 My dad built me a _____ at the bottom of the garden.

MAKE, LET & ALLOW

3 Choose the correct word to complete the sentences.

1 The prison guards *make / let* us play music until 10pm.
2 The prison *allows / lets* us to have one hour's exercise outside a day.
3 The prison doesn't *make / allow* us to smoke in our cells.
4 Prison regulations *let / make* us work hard ten hours a day.
5 If a prisoner wants to take exams, prison regulations *let / allow* them study for two hours a day.
6 They *allow / let* family and friends visit us regularly.
7 The prison guards *make / let* us surf the internet, watch TV or play games after dinner.
8 They *make / allow* us go back to our cells at 8.30 at night.

TRANSLATION

4 Translate the sentences into your language.

1 Some people prefer rented accommodation to buying a house.

_____.

2 The owners don't allow smoking in the flat, but you can smoke in the garden.

_____.

3 I want to sell my flat in the town centre and move out to the suburbs.

_____.

4 Our holiday home allows us to spend four months a year in Italy.

_____.

5 The owners make you pay a two-month deposit before you can move in.

_____.

3c | Bedrooms

VERB COLLOCATIONS (SLEEP)

1 Complete the dialogue between a doctor (D) and her patient (P) with words from the box.

feel	set	get	wake	nap	fall

D: Take a seat, Mrs Patel. Now what seems to be the matter?

P: I'm always tired, doctor. If I sit on the sofa for more than five minutes, I (1) _____ asleep.

D: Oh, dear. How much sleep do you get?

P: Not enough. I go to bed at eleven, but I don't
(2) _____ to sleep before one. I
(3) _____ my alarm clock for six, but I
(4) _____ up at five.

D: I see. Have you tried having a (5) _____ during the day?

P: I should because I always (6) _____ sleepy.

D: Uh-huh. Mrs Patel, I think you have to … Mrs Patel? Mrs Patel! Wake up …

MODALS OF OBLIGATION, PERMISSION & PROHIBITION (PAST TIME)

2 Complete the text with *were allowed to, weren't allowed to, had to, didn't need to, didn't have to* or *could*.

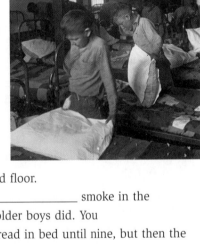

I went to a strict boarding school with rules for everything. Take, for example, the bedrooms. You
(1) _____
make your beds and keep the room clean and tidy, although of course you
(2) _____
clean the windows and floor. Obviously, you (3) _____ smoke in the bedrooms, but some older boys did. You
(4) _____ read in bed until nine, but then the lights were turned off. Sundays were more relaxed. You
(5) _____ wake up until eight and there were no lessons. You were free and you (6) _____ do what you wanted. Sunday was always my favourite day.

3 Choose the correct phrases to complete the dialogue between a granddaughter (GD) and a grandmother (GM).

GD: Gran, did you have to study for exams?

GM: Oh, yes. Children have always had tests and exams. But you're a lot luckier these days.

GD: Luckier? Why?

GM: Well, we (1) *didn't have to / had to* do so much housework. And our parents were much stricter.

GD: Do you mean that you (2) *could / had to* be home by six, or something?

GM: We (3) *were allowed to / had to* be home before it got dark. You can go out till ten or eleven!

GD: Yeah. But weren't you allowed to do anything?

GM: Of course. Generally speaking, we (4) *had to / were allowed to* do what we wanted. Parents weren't worried about children being hit by cars or attacked. We (5) *were not allowed to / could* walk out of the door on Saturday morning and come back at teatime and our parents didn't say a word.

GD: Fantastic.

GM: Yes. And we (6) *didn't have to / had to* worry so much about fashion – that's a terrible pressure nowadays.

GD: Yeah. But didn't you get dressed up for parties and stuff?

GM: No. I only had one party dress! So I (7) *had to / didn't need to* worry about that.

VOCABULARY FROM THE LESSON

4 Underline the word or phrase that does not go with the verb.

1 **make**   a bed   complain   a decision   a record
2 **have**   rules   a conviction for drugs   sleepy   a cold
3 **be**   a heavy sleeper   fresh and airy   sleepy   peace   a chance
4 **get**   a visa for America   a good night's sleep   up in the morning   a disagreement
5 **go**   through passport control   nowhere   bed   home

🔘 DICTATION

5 🔘 11 Write the sentences that you hear.

1 _____.

2 _____.

3 _____.

4 _____.

5 _____.

3D | Dinner invitation

REQUESTS

1 Read the situations and choose the correct phrase to complete the sentences.

1 You're having something to eat at a friend's house. Ask him to pass you the salt.
Do you mind / Can you pass me the salt?

2 You're in a newsagent's and you want to buy a magazine. What do you say?
Do I / Can I buy this magazine, please?

3 A work colleague lives next to the post office. Ask her to post a letter for you.
Could you possibly / Would you mind posting this letter for me?

4 You really need to take a day off work tomorrow. Ask your boss.
I wonder if I could / Do you think you could take the day off tomorrow?

5 You're in a train carriage and it's very hot. Ask the lady opposite you if it is OK to open the window.
Would you mind if I / Do you think I could opened the window? It's very hot.

6 You're late and need a lift to the station. Ask your friend if she can take you.
Do you / Could you give me a lift to the station?

'Could you possibly…?'

2 Find and correct the mistake in each dialogue.

1 **Thomas:** Can I used your toilet?
Catriona: Yes, certainly.

2 **Pierre:** Could you telling me how to get to Piccadilly Gardens?
Mavis: No problem. It's straight ahead, past that school on the corner.

3 **Erika:** Is it alright if I to close this door? It's too noisy.
Tom: Yes, of course.

4 **Victoria:** Could I borrow your pen? Mine's at home.
Marion: I'm afraid you can. I'm using it.

5 **Chris:** Did you think you could lend me £5?
Douglas: I'm sorry, but I haven't been paid yet.

6 **Lou:** Is it alright if I gone to bed early? I'm very tired.
Andrew: Yes, go ahead.

3 Look again at dialogues 1–6 in exercise 2. Decide which are requests for permission (P) and which are requests for someone else to do something (D).

1 _____   2 _____   3 _____

4 _____   5 _____   6 _____

TRANSLATION

4 Translate the dialogue into your language.

Marjory: I wonder if I could leave my coat somewhere?
Frank: Feel free. There's a wardrobe in the bedroom. Do you need any help?
Marjory: Would you mind opening the door for me?
Frank: No worries. Just leave it there.
Marjory: OK. Thanks. Is it alright if I use this hanger?
Frank: Sure. Be my guest.

_____

_____

_____

_____

_____

_____

3 | Reading

1 Read the magazine article and choose the best title 1–3.

1 A life of no responsibility
2 A life of luxury
3 A travelling life

2 Read the article again and write question letters a–d in the correct spaces 1–4 in the text.

a What's it like living in such a small space?
b Do you ever have problems with local people or the police?
c Why did you choose this lifestyle?
d Do you work?

3 Decide if the sentences are true (T) or false (F). Correct the false sentences.

1 Mark has travelled all over the world. ___
2 The most important thing for Mark is the right to do what he wants. ___
3 He often has problems with residents or the police. ___
4 He doesn't think people have to work. ___
5 'WWOOFs' are paid money for their work. ___
6 He doesn't mind living in a small place. ___

4 Find words or phrases in the article which mean the same as the definitions below. The paragraph numbers are in brackets.

1 a place where you always live (1) _____
2 limitations (2) _____
3 to annoy someone or cause them problems (3) _____
4 cut in a violent way (3) _____
5 popular performances of music that DJs do for money (4) _____
6 things (5) _____

🔊 READ & LISTEN

5 🔊 **12** Listen to Reading 3 on the CD and read the article again.

INTERVIEW

I
Mark Westgate is a traveller, that is to say, someone who lives on the road and doesn't have a fixed abode. For over 30 years he has lived in buses and coaches and visited every continent on the planet. His latest home is a small van that is just two metres wide and six metres long. I went to meet him and ask him a few questions.

Interviewer: (1) _____
2
Mark: The most important thing for me is freedom – freedom from the constraints that most people have, like a house and a steady job. I can move when and where I want to. Travel has allowed me to meet people and experience new cultures. I think my lifestyle is a reaction to my parents. They controlled me and I wasn't allowed to do a lot of things other children did.

Interviewer: (2) _____
3
Mark: No, not really. If you respect people, things are normally fine. The police make me move on from time to time, but that's OK – they have to do their job, too. People hassle me sometimes – you know, by saying that I shouldn't park somewhere, or that I should go back to my own country. I once woke up to find that I had two flat tyres because someone had slashed them during the night. But bad experiences like that are very, very rare.

Interviewer: (3) _____
4
Mark: Of course. I believe everyone has to do something. I'm a travelling DJ and I do gigs all over Europe – mostly for the peace movement or for friends. I also work as a 'WWOOF' – that's a 'Willing Worker On Organic Farms'. The workers aren't paid, but are given food and accommodation. The farmers always let me park my van in a field.

Interviewer: (4) _____
5
Mark: It's great! Everything is relative, isn't it? When I was a child, I had an enormous bedroom, but I wasn't happy. Now I live in one small room on wheels and I am very happy. The space doesn't worry me. I have to be organized, but I don't have much stuff and I'm a tidy person. My van is my bedroom, lounge, kitchen and bathroom. Sadly, I don't have a shower, but I am thinking of building a swimming pool under my bed.

4A | Luck of the draw

PAST SIMPLE & PAST CONTINUOUS

1 Choose the best verb form to complete the sentences.

1 Jack was looking for a job when he *was winning / won* the lottery.
2 I *was crossing / crossed* the road, went into the shop and bought a lottery ticket.
3 I *was watching / watched* a game of tennis when my boyfriend phoned and told me I'd won £25,000.
4 I *was buying / bought* my lottery ticket on Saturday and as usual I didn't win a thing.
5 The gambling industry *was making / made* over £42 billion last year.
6 I *was listening / listened* to the radio when my winning numbers came up.
7 My sister *was living / lived* on nothing when she won £1,000,000.
8 I *was reading / read* the newspaper when I saw an article about an old school friend of mine who had won £12 million.

2 Complete the text with the correct form of the verbs in brackets.

My friend (1) _____ (*tell*) me a funny story the other day. When she was at university, she (2) _____ (*share*) a house with five other girls and none of them had any money. One day, they (3) _____ (*talk*) about ways to make money when one of them (4) _____ (*suggest*) they buy a lottery ticket. They (5) _____ (*decide*) to use the dates they were born as their 'lottery numbers'. The next Saturday, they (6) _____ (*sit*) in a café and (7) _____ (*have*) something to drink, when the winning numbers came up on the TV. They (8) _____ (*have*) all six winning numbers. The only problem was that they had forgotten to buy a lottery ticket!

VOCABULARY FROM THE LESSON

3 Complete the dialogue with words or phrases from the box.

> scratchcards   jackpot   raise money   charities
> a lot at stake   against the odds   win the lottery

Alf: This is serious. The club now owes the bank £250,000. There's (1) _____ here. No money means no football club!

Brian: £250,000! How on earth can we (2) _____ of that sort?

Charlie: Easy! Rob a bank or (3) _____.

Alf: Our chances of winning the lottery are one in three million – totally (4) _____.

Charlie: How about (5) _____? I like them because you know straight away if you've won or not.

Brian: I've got an idea … maybe there are some (6) _____ that help sports clubs.

Alf: We're hardly a priority, are we? But maybe we could find a local business to sponsor …

Brian: Wait a second! Jason … Jason Sewell.

**Alf &
Charlie:** From school?

Brian: Yeah. He won a lottery (7) _____ worth £7 million ten years ago. He's a billionaire now and a big football fan.

Charlie: Terrific! He's our man.

⊙ DICTATION

4 ⊙ **13** Write the story that you hear.

_____

_____

_____

_____

_____

_____

_____

⊙ READ & LISTEN

5 ⊙ **14** Read and listen to *Lottery winners and losers* on page 36 of the Student's Book.

4B | Twists of fate

PAST PERFECT SIMPLE

1 Look at these sentences. Write *1* by the action that happened first and *2* by the action that happened after it.

1 *When I got to the station* (2), *the train had already left.* (1)
2 She'd already left ( ) by the time I got to the party. ( )
3 The moment I opened the door, I saw ( ) that someone had broken into the flat. ( )
4 I didn't recognize her at first ( ) because she'd changed her hairstyle and hair colour. ( )
5 Unfortunately, we got to the cinema ( ) after the film had started. ( )
6 The football match was so bad that half the fans had left ( ) before the game finished. ( )
7 I'd read and replied to 87 emails ( ) by the time I stopped for lunch. ( )

2 Choose the correct verb forms to complete the story.

On August 1, Martin Wallis and Bob Cram (1) *went / had gone* to the Accident and Emergency Department of Sutton Hospital. Mr Wallis (2) *broke / had broken* his arm and burned himself badly. Mr Cram (3) *twisted / had twisted* his ankle, sprained his wrist and broken his nose.

Apparently, the two men had entered Mr Wallis' flat earlier in the day to do some DIY work. Mr Cram turned on the gas and was looking for some matches when he (4) *put / had put* his foot in a bucket of water that the cleaner (5) *left / had left* there earlier. He (6) *skidded / had skidded* across the kitchen and (7) *grabbed / had grabbed* at one of the kitchen wall units to stop his fall. Unfortunately, being a rather large man, he pulled all three wall units off the wall as he fell down.

Then Mr Wallis, hearing the commotion, (8) *entered / had entered* the kitchen with a lit cigarette in his mouth. The gas from the cooker instantly (9) *ignited / had ignited*. The explosion threw Mr Wallis across the room and burned all of his hair off. Luckily, Mr Cram was protected from the explosion because he (10) *was / had been* under the wall units.

INJURIES

3 Complete the dialogues with injuries from the box.

> suffering   bleeding   black eye   sprained
> unconscious   twisted   scratches   bruise

1 **A:** Why can't you play football?
   B: Because I _____ my ankle.
2 **A:** Mum, I fell off my bike.
   B: I can see that, darling. You've got a big black _____ on your leg.
3 **A:** You're _____!
   B: Yes, I cut my finger when I was peeling the potatoes.
4 **A:** I think he's _____ from shock.
   B: Yes, he is. He's just received some very bad news.
5 **A:** She can't hear you, can she?
   B: No, that car just knocked her down and she's _____.
6 **A:** You've got _____ on your arm.
   B: Yes, it was that stupid cat!
7 **A:** Are you playing tennis on Saturday?
   B: I'm afraid I can't. I _____ my wrist.
8 **A:** How did he get that _____?
   B: Oh, he was in a fight.

🔊 DICTATION

4 🔊 **15** Write the sentences that you hear.

1 _____.
2 _____.
3 _____.
4 _____.

4c | Bad luck stories

TIME LINKERS

1 Choose the best time linker to complete the sentences.

1 Kate phoned *the moment / while* you were having a bath.
2 *The moment / While* I found the bag, I phoned the police.
3 I'd had three different job offers *while / by the time* I left my old job.
4 *While / As soon as* they met, they fell in love.
5 *As / By the time* I was driving to Cornwall, the countryside became more beautiful and green.

2 Read the two articles. Find and correct six mistakes with time linkers. More than one answer is possible.

A couple decided to go away for the weekend in their motor home. By the time they were taking a walk, a thief paid them a visit. While they got back, they noticed that something was wrong, so they took a look around. They found a man in the bushes being violently sick. It appeared that the thief had tried to steal petrol from the motor home using suction and a plastic tube. Unfortunately, he'd connected the tube to the toilet tank instead of the petrol tank. As soon as the police arrived, the ambulance had already taken the thief away.

Two ten-year-old girls were seriously reprimanded by the police yesterday for playing tricks on customers of the Garden Café in Swansea. The girls would wait while customers ate their sandwiches. While they threw away the plastic boxes the sandwiches came in, the girls would secretly refill them with 'new' sandwiches made of grass, leaves and flowers. The two would then go into the café and by the time the staff weren't looking, they would put the 'new' sandwiches back on the cool shelves. The girls would then go back outside and watch as customers ate their sandwiches. Kate Waters and Pia Fine said they were sorry and hadn't wanted to hurt anybody. They confessed, 'It was so funny to watch the faces of people as they tried the sandwiches. One man had eaten half a sandwich the moment he noticed he was eating grass.'

VOCABULARY FROM THE LESSON

3 Complete the bad luck stories with words from the box. Write the verbs in the correct form.

| lock out | cut off | get away |
| hang out | jump onto | put on |

1 The moment Sophie Miller _____ her washing _____ to dry, a huge lorry drove by and covered the washing with dirt …
2 As Penny Fisher was leaving a lift, the doors closed and her long ponytail was caught between the doors. She had to _____ _____ her hair with her nail scissors to escape …
3 Thieves who stole over $10,000 worth of diamonds believed they had _____ _____ with their crime until police identified them from CCTV footage …
4 The moment Patrick Hughes walked out through the front door in his pyjamas to pick up his post, a gust of wind blew the door shut and _____ him _____. He had no key and had to wait five hours until his wife came home …
5 Doreen Smith had spent hours laying the table for Christmas dinner. Five minutes before the guests arrived, her cat _____ _____ the table, knocked over a bottle of wine, and ruined everything …
6 On her way to an interview, Molly Clarke tried to _____ her make-up _____ while she was travelling on the underground. The train stopped suddenly and she had lipstick all over her face …

TRANSLATION

4 Translate the sentences into your language.

1 I was running for the bus when I fell over and twisted my ankle.

_____.

2 Christine and I had been married for eighteen months when Richard was born.

_____.

3 By the time I returned to the kitchen, the children had eaten all the cake.

_____.

4 It suddenly started to rain when they were walking in the park.

_____.

5 When I got home, I realized that I had left my keys in the office.

_____.

4D | Fancy that!

BOTH & NEITHER

1 Complete the online chat room dialogue with words and phrases from the box.

> We're both from Edinburgh   neither of us liked
> Neither did I   I do
> Both of us are divorced   both of us

ladybug187: Hi, superchap.

superchap249: Hi, ladybug. Where are you from?

ladybug187: I'm originally from Scotland.

superchap249: Oh, really? So (1) _____ are Scottish. Whereabouts?

ladybug187: Edinburgh.

superchap249: Wow! (2) _____. Do you still live there?

ladybug187: No. I moved to York and then to Birmingham.

superchap249: What a coincidence! I used to live in York, but I'm in Bristol now. Didn't like York.

ladybug187: (3) _____. It wasn't a good time of my life.

superchap249: So, (4) _____ York.

ladybug187: Crazy! So, do you have any hobbies?

superchap249: I used to play a lot of tennis, until I got divorced.

ladybug187: You're divorced? So am I! (5) _____.

superchap249: No fun is it? Still, at least I don't have to play tennis anymore. I don't like tennis.

ladybug187: (6) _____. Your name is Jerry, isn't it?

superchap249: Yes. How did you know that!?

ladybug187: We were married for ten years, you idiot!

2 Complete the table using the dialogue in exercise 1 to help you.

Prompt	Both superchap and ladybug	Neither superchap or ladybug	Only superchap	Only ladybug
(1) From Scotland?	✓			
(2) From Edinburgh?				
(3) Lived in York?				
(4) Liked York?				
(5) Moved to Birmingham?				
(6) Moved to Bristol?				
(7) Divorced?				
(8) Like tennis?				

TALKING ABOUT SIMILARITIES & DIFFERENCES

3 Match the sentences 1–6 to the responses a–f.

1 I've just won something on the lottery!
2 This time last year, I was celebrating the win.
3 That looks horrible. I'm not eating that.
4 I've never won a penny on the lottery.
5 I can't understand people who gamble.
6 My parents allowed me to smoke when I was fourteen.

- [ ] a No, neither am I.
- [ ] b So was I. Weren't we lucky!
- [ ] c I can. I was addicted to it once.
- [ ] d That's incredible! So have I.
- [ ] e Really! Mine didn't.
- [ ] f No, neither have I. It's such a waste of money.

4 Choose the incorrect response to the first sentences.

1 **A:** I didn't go to the cinema on Friday.
  B: *Neither did I. / Neither didn't I. / Me neither.*
2 **A:** I saw the new Brad Pitt film on Saturday.
  B: *So do I. / Me, too. / So did I.*
3 **A:** I love chocolate.
  B: *Me, too. / I too. / I don't.*
4 **A:** I haven't seen Tom for ages.
  B: *Neither I have. / I have. / Me, neither.*
5 **A:** I'm reading Harry Potter.
  B: *Me, too. / So I am. / I'm not.*
6 **A:** I can't understand the problem.
  B: *I can. / Neither can I. / I can, too.*

TRANSLATION

5 Translate the text into your language.

I was living in Warsaw when I first met Kasia. She was sitting in a café and we just started chatting. It was small talk at first: 'I don't like the traffic.' 'Neither do I.' 'I have a brother.' 'So do I.' But there were some real coincidences. For example, both of us were born in the same year, on the same day and in the same hospital. And neither of us had ever fallen in love. And all that was 40 years ago.

_____

_____

_____

_____

_____

_____

4 | Reading

A WIN ON THE HORSES

1 _____

Horse racing is big business in the UK. There are a number of race meetings on every single day of the week, and thousands of people attend the biggest meetings. National Hunt racing, in which the horses jump over fences, takes place from autumn to spring, whereas the Flat racing season starts in the spring and ends before the winter. Both types of racing attract professional gamblers who are experts at understanding the form of the horses and playing the odds. However, they also attract ordinary people who go to the races with friends and enjoy trying their luck even though they usually lose.

2 _____

Steve Whiteley, a heating engineer in his sixties, was just one of those ordinary people when he headed to the racecourse in Exeter with seven of his friends in March, 2011. However, by the time the day was over, Steve had won the biggest jackpot in horse racing history and was £1.4 million richer. What was even more amazing was that on the day of the win he very nearly didn't go to the race meeting because he was a bit short of money. He only decided to go when he realized that entrance to the racecourse was free on that day and he could use his bus pass to get to the meeting without having to pay anything!

3 _____

Steve's winning bet was fairly complicated. He didn't just place money on one horse to win. There were six horse races at Exeter on that day, and he chose which horse he thought would win each race. He then placed a £2 bet on this happening. He needed all six horses he had selected to win their races before he won any money. Of course, the odds against predicting the winners of all six races were huge. That was why he won so much when, amazingly, every single horse passed the finishing line in first place.

4 _____

As soon as the sixth horse had won, Steve became a celebrity. Everybody at the racecourse was cheering him, and journalists were keen to interview him. They asked him what his secret was, but, of course, he didn't have one. He explained that he had chosen the winning horses at random. For example, the winner of the fourth race had the same name as a friend of his, and the winner of the fifth race was named after a town he knew. When journalists asked him what he intended to do with the money, Steve explained that his first priority was to buy a present for his girlfriend because it was her birthday. Before the race meeting, he hadn't had enough money for a present, so he had only got her a card! Now, she could look forward to something special!

---

1 Read the article. Match the headings a–d to the paragraphs 1–4.

a The man who won £1.4 million
b How to pick a winner
c The popularity of horse racing
d How Steve's bet worked

2 Read the article again and choose the correct answer, a or b.

1 Which type of racing takes place during the winter months in the UK?
  a) National Hunt
  b) Flat
2 What type of people tend to go to Flat racing?
  a) mostly professional gamblers
  b) all types of people
3 Why did Steve almost miss the day at Exeter racecourse?
  a) He didn't have much money.
  b) He thought he had to work that day.
4 How much did it cost Steve to go to the races in the end?
  a) It didn't cost anything.
  b) It only cost him his bus fare.
5 How many races did Steve win in order to become a millionaire?
  a) just the one
  b) six in a row
6 How did he choose the horses that he placed the bet on?
  a) He chose horses with good form.
  b) He chose horses with names he recognized.
7 What had Steve bought his girlfriend for her birthday before he won £1.4 million?
  a) just a card
  b) a cheap present

3 Find words or phrases in the text that mean the same as the definitions 1–9. The paragraph numbers are in brackets.

1 go to (1)
2 appeal to (1)
3 not unusual (2)
4 went to (2)
5 not simple (3)
6 selected (3)
7 shouting and saying 'well done' (4)
8 enthusiastic (4)
9 in no order or for no reason (4)

🔊 READ & LISTEN

4 🔊 **16** Listen to Reading 4 *A win on the horses* on the CD and read the article again.

5A | Hard sell

Adjectives (advertising)

1 Match the adjectives from the box to the products 1–6.

| comfortable delicious efficient fashionable healthy popular reliable strong stylish |

1 furniture _____
2 a car _____
3 food _____
4 clothes _____
5 a washing machine _____

2 Complete the sentences with the adjectives from exercise 1.

1 *Triton Trainers* are so _____ to wear that your feet will feel warm and relaxed all day.

2 *Cherokee Cycles* sells more bikes than anyone else! We're the world's most _____ bike manufacturer.

3 *Sheng Cheng Hong* restaurant has tasteful, modern, elegant décor. In fact, it's one of the most _____ restaurants in London.

4 The *Country Cruiser* is a car that will never break down and will always start in the morning. It's an extremely _____ vehicle. Test drive one today!

5 At Dovey Accountancy, we are professional, well-organized and do everything on time. We are a very _____ company.

6 *Brady Boots* are new and have come straight from the shows in Paris. All the film stars are wearing them. They are so _____!

Comparisons 1

3 Match the adjectives 1–8 to the nouns and noun phrases a–d.

1 short
2 heavy
3 cheap
4 big   a size
5 small   b battery life
6 light   c weight
7 long   d price
8 expensive

4 Read the review of two smartphones. Complete the sentences comparing the phones using the adjectives 1–8 in exercise 3.

File   Edit   View   Favourites   Tools   Help   Links ➤

WHICH SMARTPHONE?

This week's latest smartphones

▶ **XTC Wave**

Battery life: 18 hours
Weight: 0.15 kilos
Size: 12 x 8 cm
Price: £50

Expert's view: ★ ★ ★ stars

▶ **OMD Cloud**

Battery life: 12 hours
Weight: 0.18 kilos
Size: 11 x 7 cm
Price: £80

Expert's view: ★ ★ ★ ★ stars

1 The XTC Wave lasts _____.
2 The OMD Cloud is _____.
3 The XTC Wave is _____.
4 The OMD Cloud is _____.
5 The XTC Wave is _____.
6 The experts think the OMD Cloud is

_____

🔘 Dictation

5 🔘 **17** Write the sentences that you hear.

1 _____.
2 _____.
3 _____.
4 _____.
5 _____.

🔘 Read & listen

6 🔘 **18** Read and listen to the reading text *Catch them young* on page 46 of the Student's Book.

5B | Cold calling

COMPARISONS 2

1 Rewrite the sentences using the appropriate form of the word in brackets so that the meaning is the same.

1 No other cereal bars are as good as *Super cereal* bars. (*good*)
   Super cereal bars are better than any other cereal bars.

2 Other cereal bars are not as fruity as *Super cereal* bars.
   Super cereal bars are _____.
   (*fruity*)

3 *Super cereal* bars are not the same as other cereal bars.
   Super cereal bars are _____.
   (*different*)

4 *Super cereal* bars are the healthiest bars on the market.
   No other cereal bar is _____.
   (*healthy*)

5 Other cereal bars are not as popular with children.
   Super cereal bars are _____.
   (*popular*)

6 *Super cereal* bars are the least expensive you can buy.
   No other cereal bar is _____.
   (*cheap*)

2 Correct the mistake in each sentence.

1 Branded trainers are often the same quality that normal trainers, but just more expensive.
2 I don't think that your mobile is so good as mine.
3 Yuck! That fizzy drink is not as best as *Koola Kola*!
4 That new digital camera isn't very different of the older version.
5 I think the new XP3 smartphone is much gooder than the XP2.
6 Why did you buy that DVD player? It's very similar the one you already have.

ADJECTIVES (NEGATIVE PREFIXES)

3 Complete the table with the adjectives from the box.

> ~~believable~~   sufficient   patient   lucky
> prepared   honest   successful   accurate
> polite   correct   convenient   satisfied

dis-	un- *unbelievable*	im-	in

4 Complete the sentences with a negative adjective from exercise 3. Not all the adjectives are used.

1 I'm sorry to phone so late. Is it an _____ time?

2 I buy lottery tickets all the time, but I never win anything. I'm very _____.

3 Does advertising tell the truth? No way. Most of it is _____.

4 I told him I didn't want another credit card and he hung up. How _____!

5 I'm very _____ with the service you offer, so I'm going to find another bank.

6 I was _____ for the exam, so I didn't pass it.

7 Please just wait for a second! You are so _____ at times.

8 Unfortunately, his attempt to reach Antarctica on foot was _____.

TRANSLATION

5 Translate the sentences into your language.

1 Advertisers are very aware of the fact that girls are much bigger spenders than boys.

   _____.

2 This mp3 player's hard drive isn't nearly as big as the other one.

   _____.

3 Children are one of the most important markets for advertisers.

   _____.

4 When I was a child, advertising was much less sophisticated than it is now.

   _____.

5c | The office

COMPARING NOUNS

1 Choose the correct words to complete the dialogue between Alison (A) and Barbara (B).

A: So, who should we promote?
B: Well, who has the (1) *most / more* experience, Simon or Kate?
A: Simon, definitely. He's the (2) *long / longest* serving member of staff.
B: True. But is he the (3) *good / best* person for the job?
A: Well, I think so. He's one of the (4) *hardly / hardest* workers in the department; he works (5) *longest / longer* hours than anyone else.
B: Yes, I agree with all of that. I'm not sure those are the (6) *more / most* important qualities at the moment though. I feel this new job is for someone who has (7) *more / the most* vision than the rest; and someone who can make the right decisions and make them quickly.
A: So you don't feel Simon is right for the job?
B: To be honest, no. Kate is different though. I've been watching her. OK, she's made a couple of bad decisions, but she's the (8) *quick / quickest* learner I've seen for years. She's also made the best decisions in the team.
A: Simon is the most popular person in the team.
B: He is. But does that make him a leader? He's (9) *lesser / less* respected than Kate, don't you think?
A: True. And he tends to shy away from leadership.
B: Yes, I agree.

OFFICE ACTIVITIES

2 Complete the sentences with a noun or phrase from the box. Remember to put the verbs in the correct form!

> make   write   receive   make   send   make
> report   phone calls   photocopies   coffee
> emails   call

1 I'm going to the kitchen. Can I _____ you a _____?
2 I'll _____ a detailed _____ and have it on your desk first thing Monday morning, sir.

3 Could you _____ me five double-sided _____ of this letter, please?
4 I've just arrived back from holiday to find 231 _____ have been _____ to me while I was away.
5 I'm sorry, I have to go now. I've just _____ an urgent _____ from the hospital.
6 While I'm flying I won't be able to _____ any _____, so I'll contact you when I get there, OK?

VOCABULARY FROM THE LESSON

3 Complete the sentences with a word or phrase from the box.

> get some work experience   colleagues
> at my desk   a staff   cell phone
> laptop   boss   9 to 5

1 I wish I had an exciting job, not just a regular Monday to Friday _____.
2 My work _____ are great fun, but the _____ is an idiot.
3 She works from home a lot, but she'll pick up your emails on her _____ or you could ring her on her _____.
4 I'm off for lunch but will be back _____ by 2pm.
5 Yeah, it's a pretty small company. We've only got _____ of eleven, but we're growing fast.
6 I'm here for six weeks to _____ before I go to university.

DICTATION

4 🔊 **19** Write the sentences that you hear.

1 _____.
2 _____?
3 _____.
4 _____.
5 _____.

READ & LISTEN

5 🔊 **20** Read and listen to the reading text *Office Stereotypes* on page 50 of the Student's Book.

5D | Paperwork

OFFICE SUPPLIES

1 Find ten office objects in the word search.

n	o	d	a	p	a	p	e	r	c	l	i	p	u	p
f	y	r	l	o	x	i	w	a	u	c	n	e	z	d
a	m	u	k	r	s	d	h	i	p	y	g	n	r	h
p	t	b	i	r	o	m	r	u	t	h	a	c	l	i
z	a	b	n	e	k	g	o	p	i	n	k	i	a	g
t	i	e	k	s	v	r	i	s	k	s	b	l	o	h
o	g	r	c	r	t	g	u	d	p	e	x	s	e	l
d	r	e	a	m	s	l	o	g	h	l	g	h	y	i
h	i	t	r	u	g	p	m	o	n	l	d	a	b	g
p	o	s	t	i	t	s	a	t	w	o	b	r	i	h
l	f	u	r	m	r	o	s	e	w	t	i	p	e	t
f	e	t	i	p	p	e	x	r	n	a	x	e	t	e
m	o	r	d	r	a	w	i	n	g	p	i	n	s	r
a	p	u	g	e	j	i	n	o	b	e	r	e	t	a
n	o	t	e	p	a	d	g	r	e	y	t	r	i	p

ON THE PHONE

2 Complete the phone dialogue between a caller (C) and a secretary (S) with sentences or phrases from the box.

> Could you tell him   will he be back in the office
> Could I take a message
> I don't think he'll be back until tomorrow morning
> I'll call back then   Could you say that again

C: Could I speak to Mr Vaswani, please?
S: I'm afraid he's not in the office this morning.
  (1) _____?
C: Yes, please. (2) _____ Mr Chowdri phoned?
S: I'm sorry. (3) _____, please? I'm afraid it's a bad line.
C: Yes, it is, isn't it? The name's Chowdri. C-H-O-W-D-R-I.
S: Thank you, Mr Chowdri.
C: When (4) _____?
S: (5) _____.
C: Tomorrow morning? OK, (6)_____.
S: Thank you, Mr Chowdri. I'll tell him you called. Goodbye.

3 Read the telephone dialogue between a caller (C) and a secretary (S). Why does the secretary seem to be unfriendly?

C: I want to speak to Ms Horne.
S: Who's calling, please?
C: John Stratford from Stratford Cars.
S: I'm sorry, but Ms Horne's not at her desk. Would you like to leave a message?
C: Yes. Tell her to call me.
S: Excuse me!?
C: Get her to call me when she gets back, OK?
S: Well … yes. Do you have a number?
C: Yes. It's 0267 3416.
S: 0267 3416?
C: That's right.
S: I'll pass the message on.
C: Good.

4 Underline the parts of the dialogue that seem impolite. Rewrite them so that they are more polite than the original.

TRANSLATION

5 Translate the telephone dialogue into your language.

A: Could I speak to Ms Harvey, please?
B: I'm afraid she's not in the office at the moment.
A: Do you know when she'll be back?
B: I think she'll be back tomorrow morning. Can I take a message for her?
A: No. I'll call her tomorrow. Thank you.
B: You're welcome. Goodbye.
A: Goodbye.

_____

_____

_____

_____

_____

5 | Reading

1 Match the words 1–5 to the definitions a–e.

1	takeaway food	a	money that you spend on something
2	stationery	b	sweets and chocolate
3	fare	c	ready-to-eat food that you take away from a restaurant
4	expenditure	d	things that you use to write with, like paper and pens
5	confectionery	e	the price you pay to travel on a bus, train, etc

2 Look at this quiz for parents of seven to fifteen-year-olds in the UK. The quiz asks them about their children's expenditure per week in the UK. Can you guess the answers?

Do you really know what your kids spend their money on?

❶ Seven to fifteen-year-olds spend an average of
a) £10.70 b) £12.00 c) £11.40 a week.

❷ Boys spend a) more money than b) less money than
c) the same amount of money as girls a week.

❸ The biggest expenditure for boys and girls is …
a) bus and train fares. b) clothes and shoes.
c) takeaway food and snacks.

❹ The smallest expenditure for boys and girls is on …
a) confectionery and snacks. b) fares.
c) mobile phones and charges.

❺ The two areas that boys and girls spend the same
amount of money on are … a) sporting and cultural
activities, music accessories. b) fares, sporting and
cultural activities. c) mobile phones and charges,
takeaway and snack food.

3 Check your answers to exercise 2 by looking at the table.

Items 7–15-year-olds spend their money on
(as a percentage of the total)

Items	Boys	Girls	All aged 7–15
takeaway and snack food eaten away from home	24%	23%	24%
clothing and footwear	12%	22%	17%
games, toys, hobbies, pets of which computer software and games	19% 12%	6% 1%	12% 6%
magazines, books and stationery	5%	6%	6%
music accessories (CDs and DVDs)	7%	4%	5%
sporting and cultural activities	4%	4%	4%
mobile phones and charges	3%	5%	4%
confectionery and snacks	3%	4%	4%
fares	2%	2%	2%
other expenditure all expenditure (=100%)	21%	24%	22%
(£ per week)	10.70	12.00	11.40

4 Complete the summary with information from exercise 3.

A year ago, a survey in the United Kingdom discovered that seven to fifteen-year-old girls spent about 12% more money than boys. Girls spent an average of £12.00 compared to £10.70 for boys. Boys and girls spent most of their money on (1) _____. Girls spent almost the same as boys: 23% and 24% respectively.

In all the other major areas except for (2) _____, children spent the same or very similar amounts of money. For example, boys spent the same as girls on sporting and cultural activities (4%) and on bus and train fares (3) _____.

The biggest difference between the two groups was in the area of games, toys, hobbies, pets. In this category (4) _____ spent much, much more on computer software and games. In fact, they spent (5) _____ of their money on these items, which was twelve times more than girls spent.

6A | Summer holiday

FUTURE 1 (FUTURE PLANS)

1 Choose the correct verb forms to complete the email.

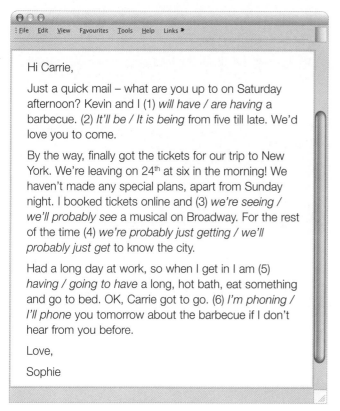

Hi Carrie,

Just a quick mail – what are you up to on Saturday afternoon? Kevin and I (1) *will have / are having* a barbecue. (2) *It'll be / It is being* from five till late. We'd love you to come.

By the way, finally got the tickets for our trip to New York. We're leaving on 24th at six in the morning! We haven't made any special plans, apart from Sunday night. I booked tickets online and (3) *we're seeing / we'll probably see* a musical on Broadway. For the rest of the time (4) *we're probably just getting / we'll probably just get* to know the city.

Had a long day at work, so when I get in I am (5) *having / going to have* a long, hot bath, eat something and go to bed. OK, Carrie got to go. (6) *I'm phoning / I'll phone* you tomorrow about the barbecue if I don't hear from you before.

Love,

Sophie

2 Read Carrie's reply to Sophie's email and correct the six mistakes in verb forms.

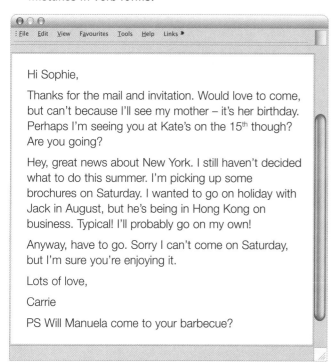

Hi Sophie,

Thanks for the mail and invitation. Would love to come, but can't because I'll see my mother – it's her birthday. Perhaps I'm seeing you at Kate's on the 15th though? Are you going?

Hey, great news about New York. I still haven't decided what to do this summer. I'm picking up some brochures on Saturday. I wanted to go on holiday with Jack in August, but he's being in Hong Kong on business. Typical! I'll probably go on my own!

Anyway, have to go. Sorry I can't come on Saturday, but I'm sure you're enjoying it.

Lots of love,

Carrie

PS Will Manuela come to your barbecue?

HOLIDAYS 1

3 Complete the dialogue between a customer (C) and a travel agent (T) with phrases from the box.

> picked up a brochure   pay a deposit
> do the packing   chosen a destination
> find your way around   book the flights

T: Travel Direct. Jenny speaking. How can I help?

C: Good morning. I (1) _____ from your travel agency yesterday.

T: OK, and have you (2) _____?

C: Yes, it's the *Bellavista Real Hotel* in the Algarve. It's on page 128.

T: Ah yes. It's a very pretty resort. Not too big, so you can (3) _____ very easily. It's a fishing village with a sandy beach.

C: Oh, that sounds lovely. Are there any family rooms for four left for the first week in August?

T: Let me just check … yes. I can reserve one for you, but you'll have to (4) _____ of 10%.

C: 10%? OK. And can I (5) _____ with you, too?

T: OK … yes, accommodation plus flights for four … that comes to £1,200.

C: Oh, great! How exciting. I think I'll (6) _____ tonight.

T: Tonight!? But the holiday doesn't start for another three months!

C: Yes, I know, but you haven't seen my shoe collection!

🔊 DICTATION

4 🔊 **21** Write the sentences that you hear.

1 _____.

2 _____.

3 _____?

4 _____.

5 _____?

6B | Getting away

Holidays 2

1 Complete the holiday advertisements with phrases from the box.

> the beaten track   laid-back atmosphere
> magnificent white beaches   cosmopolitan guests
> crowded beach parties   range of water sports
> secluded beach   exclusive, upmarket hotel
> unforgettable beach parties   picturesque mountains

Coral Retreat, Phuket ★★★★★

One of Phuket's best-kept secrets, this fabulous five-star hotel is one of the finest on the island. Set on a hill overlooking kilometres of (1) _____, the hotel sits in a beautiful coconut grove. Loved by the (2) _____ who fly in from all over the world, Coral Retreat has everything you'd expect from a five-star (3) _____. There is a wide (4) _____ such as snorkelling and sea-kayaking. The hotel also has a beautiful swimming pool, tennis courts and gym. Coral Retreat is famous for its (5) _____ on Friday night when the rich and famous dance on the sand till sunrise.

2 Match what the tourists said about their holidays 1–6 to the travel representative's replies a–f.

1 'I didn't worry about a thing while I was there. The atmosphere was so relaxing.'
2 'We've met people from all over the world here.'
3 'We sunbathed and swam and didn't see a single person all day.'
4 'I'm happy paying a lot more because it means we can avoid those horrible mass-tourist destinations.'
5 'It was hard to get here, but it's worth it to be away from the rest of the world.'
6 'I love this place because it's so pretty.'

Mermaid Beach, Mauritius ★★★

In an area said to enjoy the best weather on the island, this hotel is set on a (6) _____ that looks out to a small island. Behind and up above the hotel are the (7) _____ of the south-west coast. This small family-run hotel is off (8) _____ , so no lively clubs or (9) _____ here. Enjoy a week just relaxing in the (10) _____ – doing nothing but listening to the rhythm of the sea.

☐ a 'Yes, it's a very cosmopolitan resort, isn't it?'
☐ b 'Yes, it's a very secluded beach, isn't it?'
☐ c 'Yes, it's very laid-back, isn't it?'
☐ d 'Yes, it is off the beaten track, isn't it?'
☐ e 'Yes, it's a very picturesque village, isn't it?'
☐ f 'Yes, it's a very exclusive resort, isn't it?'

Future 2 (predictions)

3 Complete the sentences with *will* or *going to* and the verb in brackets.

1 I think I _____ (*own*) my own travel company one day.
2 Jamie has eaten all that chocolate! He _____ (*be*) sick!
3 We're already late! We _____ (*miss*) the train.
4 Don't ask me why, but, in my opinion, Simon _____ (*not / pass*) the exam.
5 Who do you think _____ (*win*) the pop talent show?
6 The boys are playing football in the garden. They _____ (*break*) a window if they aren't careful.

6c | Perfect day

PRESENT TENSES IN FUTURE TIME CLAUSES

1 Complete the description of a day trip with clauses from the box.

> you'll meet   before the coach leaves at six
> You'll have a chance   we'll take a studio tour
> you'll visit some of the   Once the tour is over

Action-packed day trip to
Universal Studios, Hollywood

Please meet in front of the hotel at ten sharp. The coach will arrive at Universal Studios at eleven. As soon as we get there, (1) _____. This is your chance to see how some of your favourite movies were made: *Jurassic Park*, *War of the Worlds* and many more. (2) _____, we'll have lunch in one of the restaurants. After lunch, (3) _____ attractions that Universal offers. We recommend the rollercoaster in *The Revenge of the Mummy*, the 4-D *Shrek* movie and the *Jurassic Park* ride where (4) _____ 'living' dinosaurs, including a 50 foot T-Rex!

(5) _____ to buy some souvenirs
(6) _____.

Enjoy the trip!

VOCABULARY FROM THE LESSON

2 Underline the word or phrase that does not go with the noun or verb.

1 **go**   out for the day   on an excursion
        on a romantic holiday   rock-climb
2 **take**   a tour of Ireland   tourists to Dublin
        drink   you for a pony ride
3 **have**   sightseeing   a look around
        lunch with friends   a swim in the sea
4 **see**   the dramatic west coast   the packing
        breathtaking scenery   a concert
5 **travel** agent's   guide   land   rep
6 **tourist** destination   attraction   resort   car

3 Complete the postcard with phrases from the box.

> holiday makers   a taste of   feel in the mood
> hire bikes   guided tour of

Dear Jude and Dave,
Having a horrible time here! On our first day we took a guided tour of churches. I'll certainly never go on one again! It was boring and the bus was hot and full of retired (1) _____ from England!

We'll probably go to a local restaurant tonight for (2) '_____ our town's best seafood'. It'll probably be fish and chips!

Tomorrow we're going on a (3) _____ the island, but I don't want to - I don't (4) _____. I'd prefer to (5) _____ and cycle around instead.

Can't wait to get home!

Love,
Your unhappy friend,

Annie xxx

DICTATION

4 🔘 **22** Write the sentences that you hear.

1 _____ .
2 _____ .
3 _____ .
4 _____ .
5 _____ .

READ & LISTEN

5 🔘 **23** Read and listen to the reading text *Emerald Tours* on page 60 of the Student's Book.

6D | Travel plans

INDIRECT QUESTIONS

1 Tick the correct questions. Correct the incorrect questions.

1 And can you tell me if that's a direct flight?
2 I wonder you have flights going from London, Heathrow to Vietnam.
3 I'd also like to know if I can book a hotel through you.
4 Do you know how long does the flight take?
5 Do you think you could tell me how much Business and Economy cost?
6 Could tell me how much do the flight costs, please?

2 Read the dialogue between a customer (C) and a travel agent (TA). Complete the dialogue with the indirect questions in exercise 1.

TA: Good morning, Freedom Travel. How may I help you?

C: Good morning. (1) _____
_____?

TA: Yes, sir. Where are you travelling to?

C: The capital, Hanoi.

TA: Yes, that's no problem.

C: Good. (2) _____
_____?

TA: Just one second. Yes, that's ... that's fifteen hours and 45 minutes with Thai Airways.

C: Oh, that's a long flight. (3) _____
_____?

TA: Bear with me ... no, sir. There's a stopover in Bangkok, Thailand. So London to Bangkok is eleven hours and 30 minutes. Then a two-and-a-half hour wait ... and then another one hour and 45 minutes to Hanoi.

C: OK. (4) _____
_____?

TA: Certainly. Return or single? First, Business or Economy, sir?

C: Return. (5) _____
_____?

TA: Sure ... just one second. Yes, here we go ... a return in Business is £1,740.90 and in Economy it's £1,050.90.

C: Oh, a big difference. I think I'll go Economy. (6) _____
_____.

TA: Yes, of course. There are a number of good hotels in Vietnam.

COLLOCATIONS WITH *SOUND*

3 Imagine someone is talking about their holiday. What would you say to the person? Choose the best option to complete the phrases.

1 And you could eat as much as you wanted for $3.00! That sounds *great / painful*.
2 We were dancing on the beach and I cut my foot on a broken bottle. That sounds *funny / painful*.
3 And at dinner this silly man talked about himself nonstop for an hour! That sounds *fascinating / boring*.
4 We sat in a hot bus for five hours. That sounds *uncomfortable / wonderful*.
5 We had dinner together and watched the sun go down. That sounds *romantic / too bad*.
6 And the guide explained how they built this 98-metre church 2,000 years ago. Wow! That sounds *much fun / fascinating*.

TRANSLATION

4 Translate the sentences into your language.

1 Could you tell me where the post office is, please?
_____?

2 Does that sound like a good idea to you?
_____?

3 Do you know what time the guided tour starts, please?
_____?

4 I'd like to know if there are any non-smoking restaurants near here.
_____.

5 Waiting for a bus for two hours doesn't sound much fun.
_____.

6 Do you think you could tell me how much a return flight costs?
_____?

6 | Reading

1 Read the article and match the paragraphs 1–4 to the headings a–d.

☐ a The real solutions
☐ b 'Carbon-neutral' tourists
☐ c The problem
☐ d A solution

WHAT IS THE REAL PRICE OF TOURISM?

1 Tourism is the largest and fastest growing industry in the world. By 2020, 1.6 billion people will be taking holidays abroad – mostly by plane. Increased flights lead to more pollution, especially the production of
5 carbon dioxide. Carbon dioxide, or CO_2, is a gas and is one of the main causes of climate change. To give an example, a return flight from London to New York creates 1.22 tonnes of the gas per person. Multiply this by the number of people flying around the world and
10 it's easy to see what a terrible effect flying has on the environment.

2 Now most of us happily take flights without realizing the damage we are causing. A small but growing number of tourists, however, are taking responsibility
15 for the CO_2 produced by their holiday. These 'carbon-neutral' travellers want to offset or 'neutralize' all the carbon dioxide their holidays produce. They do this in a number of ways, for example, by turning off air conditioning when it's not needed or asking a hotel
20 not to change towels and bedding every day. But how do you offset a return flight to New York for a family of five that produces over six tonnes of CO_2!?

3 One answer lies with a growing number of not-for-profit companies that offer to balance the negative
25 effects of CO_2 by planting trees. Trees naturally take in CO_2 and give off oxygen and this process helps to balance out the problem. So, for that return flight that produces over six tonnes of CO_2, the family gets a company to plant ten trees for them. The trees
30 neutralize the effects of the flights on the environment. It doesn't cost very much and the family, in this case, have paid the real price of their flights by becoming 'carbon-neutral'.

4 Sadly, planting trees will not solve the problem. Non-
35 governmental organizations (NGOs) like Greenpeace, an environmental pressure group, are helping by fighting for a cleaner, safer world. National governments are also acting, although they could do more. For example, they could tax airplane fuel and
40 they could get tourists to pay an 'environmental' tax. The best hope, however, lies with international organizations working together. If not, tourism will suffer. Rising sea levels are already threatening those idyllic island beach holidays and rising temperatures
45 are slowly melting the snow on those fantastic ski resorts. It's time to act!

2 Read the article again and decide if the sentences are true (T) of false (F). Correct the false sentences.

1 Planes produce CO_2, which damages the environment. ___
2 In 2020, one and a half million people will go on holiday abroad. ___
3 Most travellers know that planes are bad for the planet. ___
4 Carbon-neutral travellers want to eliminate the CO_2 they generate by flying less. ___
5 Trees help to reduce CO_2. ___
6 If you plant five trees, it neutralizes the effect of around six tonnes of CO_2. ___
7 Trees will take care of the situation. ___
8 The ultimate answer to the CO_2 problem lies with governments. ___

3 Match the speakers 1–6 to what he or she might say a–f.

1 an average tourist

2 a carbon-neutral tourist

3 a spokeswoman from an organization that works to make things better, but doesn't make any money from what they do

4 a representative from an environmental NGO

5 a government spokesperson

6 a spokesperson for an international environmental organization

a 'Governments in 141 countries have signed this agreement to reduce the production of CO_2.'

b 'I didn't know that airplanes caused so much pollution!'

c 'You don't need to change the sheets. I'm happy to use them all week during my stay.'

d 'We are going to raise taxes on all air travel.'

e 'So if you plant one tree, that will cover your return flight to Rome.'

f 'We're putting pressure on the government to stop its road-building plans.'

4 Match the words from the text 1–4 to the definitions a–d. The line numbers are in brackets.

1 offset (21)
2 tonnes (22)
3 take in (25)
4 fuel (39)

a gas or diesel used to drive a vehicle
b balance the effect of something
c absorb
d units used for measuring weight, equal to 1,000 kilograms

🎧 READ & LISTEN

5 🎧 **24** Listen to Reading 6 *What is the **real** price of tourism?* on the CD and read the article again.

7A | Moving

PRESENT PERFECT CONTINUOUS 1

1 Choose the correct verb forms to complete the email.

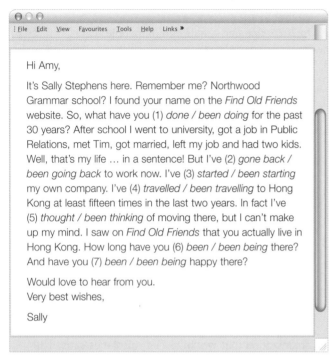

Hi Amy,

It's Sally Stephens here. Remember me? Northwood Grammar school? I found your name on the *Find Old Friends* website. So, what have you (1) *done / been doing* for the past 30 years? After school I went to university, got a job in Public Relations, met Tim, got married, left my job and had two kids. Well, that's my life … in a sentence! But I've (2) *gone back / been going back* to work now. I've (3) *started / been starting* my own company. I've (4) *travelled / been travelling* to Hong Kong at least fifteen times in the last two years. In fact I've (5) *thought / been thinking* of moving there, but I can't make up my mind. I saw on *Find Old Friends* that you actually live in Hong Kong. How long have you (6) *been / been being* there? And have you (7) *been / been being* happy there?

Would love to hear from you.
Very best wishes,

Sally

2 Read Amy's reply to Sally. Complete her email by putting the verbs in brackets into the present perfect simple or present perfect continuous.

Hi Sally,

Of course I remember you, though it (1) _____ (be) a long time! And my life? I don't know where to start. I (2) _____ (do) so many things: I've been a butcher, a baker and a belly dancer. Fifteen years ago I met a German journalist, fell in love and I (3) _____ (live) with him ever since! We moved to Berlin and I became a painter. Since then we (4) _____ (live) in nine different countries and now here we are in Hong Kong. I (5) _____ (learn) Cantonese for two years now, but it's not easy for a European. I love it here though and have made a lot of friends. As for work, I (6) _____ (paint) non-stop for six months because I've got an exhibition in December. Anyway, enough of me. Write again and let me know more about you.

Take care.

Amy

3 Complete the sentences with *for* or *since*.

1 She's been working for the bank _____ she left university.
2 I've been living out of a suitcase _____ almost a month and I'm sick of it!
3 Where have you been!? I've been waiting _____ ages!
4 She's been looking for a job _____ the company made her redundant.
5 They've lived there _____ as long as I can remember.
6 I've wanted to live in Brazil _____ I was a kid.

PHRASAL VERBS WITH *LIVE*

4 Complete the sentences with words from the box.

through	out of	for	on	up to

1 When I was young, I lived _____ a suitcase. I never stayed anywhere for very long.
2 I live _____ my pension. It's enough to buy everything I need.
3 My grandparents lived _____ the war. It was a difficult time.
4 I don't think I'll ever live _____ my parents' expectations. They want me to be very successful.
5 I live _____ my job. It's really important to me.

DICTATION

5 🔘 **25** Write the dialogue that you hear.

_____

_____

_____

_____

_____

_____

_____

_____

READ & LISTEN

6 🔘 **26** Read and listen to the reading text *Redundancy was the best thing that ever happened to me* on page 66 of the Student's Book.

7B | Life changes

METAPHOR

1 Match the metaphors 1–7 to the definitions a–g.

1	take an unexpected turn	a	become divorced or separated
2	be at a crossroads	b	change surprisingly
3	go their separate ways	c	start a new phase in life
4	embark on a new stage in life	d	change the development or progress of something
5	be no turning back	e	reach a point when you have to make an important choice in life
6	take a new direction		
7	take off	f	become successful or popular very quickly
		g	be impossible to return to a previous situation or condition

2 Match the questions 1–6 to the answers a–f.

1 'And why did you become a painter?'
2 'So was your life at a crossroads?'
3 'How long have you been divorced?'
4 'Was making such a big change in your life frightening?'
5 'Did you ever think you'd become famous?'
6 'Why did you leave the job?'

- [ ] a 'Yes, I had to make a decision. Stay or go.'
- [ ] b 'Oh, we went our separate ways about five years ago.'
- [ ] c 'I've always loved art and my life just took an unexpected turn when I lost my job.'
- [ ] d 'I was bored with it and I had the chance to embark on something new and exciting.'
- [ ] e 'Terrifying! But once I started I knew there was no turning back.'
- [ ] f 'Never, but when my second book came out, everybody bought it and my life took off.'

VOCABULARY FROM THE LESSON

3 Match the verbs 1–12 to the words they go with a–l.

1	make	a	guilty
2	miss	b	out on his childhood
3	break	c	a decision
4	feel	d	my heart
5	make	e	up a job
6	give	f	his mind
7	look	g	a change
8	change	h	after a child
9	make	i	a difficulty
10	face	j	married
11	follow	k	sense
12	get	l	a path

TRANSLATION

4 Translate the text into your language.

I've lived through a lot in my life and now I feel I'm at a crossroads. I've been thinking about what to do with the rest of my life. Become a doctor? No, I've never liked hospitals. Teacher? Maybe – I've always enjoyed the company of children. I've been talking to my mum about it and she says I've been worrying too much. She says because I'm only nine I don't need to make any big decisions yet.

PRESENT PERFECT CONTINUOUS 2

1 Choose the correct verb form to complete the sentences.

1 'Mum, Dad! Fantastic news – I've *passed / been passing*! Could I have the keys to the car to go out and celebrate tonight?'
2 'Oh, John! The flowers are so beautiful. You've *remembered / been remembering* it's my …'
3 'They've *worked / been working* hard on her dress for a couple of months, and when it's ready she'll look beautiful in white on the big day.'
4 '40 years! You know darling, I've *loved / been loving* you ever since I first met you.'
5 'They've both *done / been doing* fine, thanks. We're not getting much sleep at the moment and Rachel's really tired, but we are very, very happy.'
6 'No one *has ever worked / has ever been working* as hard as you in this company, Louise. So, I'm delighted to offer you the position.'

2 Complete the article. Put the verbs in brackets into the present perfect simple or present perfect continuous.

WINDSWEPT AND DEEP TO PART

Actress Kate Windswept and her actor husband, Johnny Deep (1) _____ (*decide*) to get divorced after seven years of marriage. Kate told our reporter, 'We (2) _____ (*experience*) a lot together: two wonderful children, dozens of films and fantastic careers, but life (3) _____ (*not / be*) easy recently. We (4) _____ (*see*) a marriage counsellor for over a year now and we (5) _____ (*argue*) non-stop for the last couple of months. So we finally decided to go our separate ways. Johnny and I (6) _____ (*talk*) to our lawyers and we are both confident that we'll stay good friends.'

3 Match what the people in exercise 1 say 1–6 to the celebrations a–f.

☐ a getting married
☐ b passing a driving test
☐ c getting a promotion
☐ d celebrating a wedding anniversary
☐ e announcing a birth
☐ f celebrating a birthday

LIFE STAGES

4 Which life stage are these people describing? Match the sentences to words from the box.

> retired   older   teenager   toddler
> thirty something   adolescent   elderly

1 'Oh, Doris is OK. She finds it hard to walk though and she can't hear very well either.' _____
2 'It's not easy making the change from being a child into an adult.' _____
3 'It's normal for a person of her age to have so many responsibilities: being a mother, taking care of her mother, being a wife, a friend, a work colleague and managing a home.' _____
4 'He's studied hard for his exams and is really looking forward to university.' _____
5 'She's just learning to walk and tries to get hold of absolutely everything!' _____
6 'He stopped working two years ago, but he's always busy. I wonder where he gets all the energy from.'

_____

🔊 DICTATION

5 🔊 **27** Write the text that you hear.

_____

_____

_____

_____

_____

_____

🔊 READ & LISTEN

6 🔊 **28** Read and listen to the reading text *Florrie prepares to celebrate her 113th birthday* on page 70 of the Student's Book.

7D | Dilemmas

EXCLAMATIONS WITH *WHAT*

1 Do the quiz. Read the questions and then choose the correct answer a–c. When you have finished, check your score at the end of the quiz.

Do you ever put your foot in it?

Saying the right thing at the right time is important if you want to make and keep friends. How good are you at doing that? Take this quiz and find out.

1 **Your friend:** What a night! Someone took my wallet with all my credit cards and money. And then I couldn't find my car keys!
   You: a) Oh, what a day!
             b) What a nightmare!
             c) What an idiot!

2 **Friend:** My company has just made 20 people redundant. I thought I was going to lose my job, too, but luckily I'm OK.
   You: a) What a shame!
             b) What a nuisance!
             c) What a relief!

3 **Friend:** My brother was caught stealing a bike.
   You: a) What an idiot!
             b) What a good idea!
             c) What a relief!

4 **Friend:** I lost my house key in the supermarket, but fortunately somebody found it and gave it to the manager. She gave it to me when I went back to the supermarket to ask about it.
   You: a) What a good idea!
             b) What a relief!
             c) What a mess!

5 **Friend:** I was in a crowded market in Mexico City and I met my first boyfriend … from primary school! He's so sweet.
   You: a) What a waste of time!
             b) What a surprise!
             c) What bad luck!

6 **Friend:** There was no time to buy a wedding cake, so we bought three cakes in different sizes and covered them in white icing. It looked great!
   You: a) What a surprise!
             b) What a waste of time!
             c) What a good idea!

Score results:
-6 to 0 = You need to listen more carefully if you want to make and keep any friends.
1 to 6 = Listen more carefully and you'll make more friends.
7 to 12 = You're a great listener and a good friend, too. Congratulations!

Scoring:
1 a) 0   b) 2   c) -1
2 a) -1 b) 0   c) 2
3 a) 2   b) -1 c) 0
4 a) -1 b) 2   c) 0
5 a) -1 b) 2   c) 0
6 a) 0   b) -1 c) 2

GIVING ADVICE

2 Complete the two dialogues with phrases from the box.

> You have to speak   If I were you,   Tell him you
> What you need to do   There's no harm in

Dialogue 1
Arec: I promised to buy a car from my neighbour, but I've just seen the same car for a much better price.
Gavin: Well, you have no choice. (1) _____ to your neighbour about it.
Arec: That would be too embarrassing.
Gavin: Well, what are you going to do? Buy the other one and park it in front of your neighbour's!? (2) _____ I'd talk to him.
Arec: But that's putting pressure on him.
Gavin: (3) _____ explaining the situation to your neighbour and he can decide.

Dialogue 2
Sylvia: I saw Tim stealing at work today.
Denise: Well, lots of people steal things from work.
Sylvia: Maybe a pencil or a biro, but not a chair!
Denise: A chair! (4) _____ saw him.
Sylvia: I couldn't tell him that!
Denise: Well, it's not right. (5) _____ is to warn him. Say that you heard someone talking about it, or something.
Sylvia: That's a good idea. Thanks!

TRANSLATION

3 Translate the advert into your language.

> Have you been waiting for your career to take off? Have others been promoted ahead of you? Maybe you are at a crossroads. But why wait? Call us now for professional career advice on 0800 007 7007.

_____

_____

_____

7 | Reading

Downshifting – a way of living

1. For the last twenty plus years, many Britons have been working harder and for longer hours than they have at any other time in Britain's history. The pressure is on to make more money and consume more. However, some have been choosing to live on a lower income and to have a simpler, less-materialistic lifestyle. This new trend is called 'downshifting' or 'voluntary simplicity'.

2. A recent survey in Britain showed that 25% of people aged between 30 and 59 have downshifted in the last ten years. That is one quarter of the working population. These people come from all walks of life, but share the feeling that something important is missing from their lives – something that money cannot provide.

3. All downshifters have been through a period when they question the purpose of their lives. They feel something is missing. When asked why they decided to make these changes, the most common answer, over 30%, was that they want to spend 'more time with the family'. Almost one in five people said they want more control over their lives and so lead fuller lives. About 13% want to have 'a healthier lifestyle' while 11% said the main reason was to achieve more balance in their lives.

4. People have downshifted in a number of different ways. Most have stopped work (30%), reduced working hours (22%) or changed careers (20%). 10% of people have taken jobs that pay less money. In fact, the average reduction in salary is a massive 40%. This salary cut normally means a dramatic change in lifestyle to a much simpler way of living.

5. Although downshifting is becoming more normal, it is still a radical decision to take and people need to plan the change carefully. If they don't, the dream they had could turn into a nightmare. The most common difficulties people have are financial ones, a lack of mental stimulation and a feeling that they are no longer valued in society. Fortunately, the majority of people are content with their decision. A massive 94% of downshifters are happy with their choice. 40% don't miss the money, 39% do and 15% say that although they are happy, the loss of money has been very difficult. Incredibly perhaps, only 6% say they are unhappy.

1 Read the article and match the paragraphs 1–5 to the headings a–e.

- ☐ a   Who 'downshifts'?
- ☐ b   How do people do it?
- ☐ c   What are the pros and cons of doing it?
- ☐ d   Why do people do it?
- ☐ e   What is it?

2 Read the article again. Match the bars 1–4 in the bar chart to the reasons a–d.

Reasons people gave for 'downshifting'

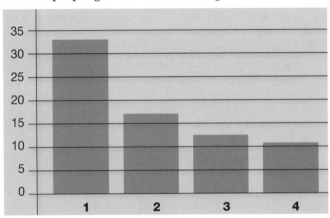

- ☐ a   to control their lives more
- ☐ b   to lead a healthier life
- ☐ c   to have a better balance in life
- ☐ d   to have more time with family

3 Write short answers to the questions.

1   How have many people in Britain been working over the last 20 or so years?

_____.

2   What is the main reason people give for downshifting?

_____.

3   What are the three main problems downshifters have?

_____.

4   What tells you that 'the majority of people are content' with their decision to downshift?

_____.

🔵 READ & LISTEN

4 🔵 **29** Listen to Reading 7 *Downshifting – a way of living* on the CD and read the article again.

8A | Breaking news

NEWSPAPERS

1 Match the words or phrases 1–8 to the definitions a–h.

1 journalist
2 headline
3 article
4 circulation
5 news coverage
6 daily
7 feature
8 press

- ☐ a a newspaper which is published every day, except Sunday
- ☐ b news about something on television, radio or in the newspapers
- ☐ c the number of copies of a newspaper or magazine that are sold or distributed
- ☐ d a newspaper or magazine article that concentrates on a particular subject
- ☐ e the title of a newspaper story, printed in large letters
- ☐ f a newspaper or magazine story
- ☐ g newspapers and news magazines, or the reporters who work on them
- ☐ h someone whose job is to report the news for a newspaper, magazine, radio or TV programme

WOULD

2 Complete the dialogue with words from the box.

never	like	'd	to be	hate	wouldn't	mind

Alan: Look at this headline: *Star attacked by four men.* I'd (1) _____ to be famous.

Bertie: So would I, but I wouldn't (2) _____ their lifestyle.

Alan: But you'd (3) _____ have any privacy.

Bertie: True. OK, I (4) _____ just have their money.

Alan: Yeah, but would you (5) _____ people asking you for money all the time?

Bertie: No, that (6) _____ be much fun.

Alan: So you wouldn't like (7) _____ rich and famous then?

Bertie: No, perhaps not.

3 Match the questions 1–6 to the answers a–f.

1 Would you like to see the news on Channel 4?
2 I'd like to work as a foreign correspondent, wouldn't you?
3 Imagine a world without newspapers. What would that be like?
4 Mum, do you think the government would ever control the news we get?
5 They say they'd pay me £60,000 a year. Would you take the job if you were me?
6 Would you ever stop buying a newspaper?

- ☐ a It'd be terrible. You would have no idea what was happening.
- ☐ b Well, some people say that they already do.
- ☐ c I'd prefer to see that film starting on ITV.
- ☐ d No, I wouldn't, but I do like reading online papers.
- ☐ e No way! It sounds exciting, but it would be far too dangerous.
- ☐ f That sounds attractive, but you'd have to work twelve hours a day, seven days a week.

TRANSLATION

4 Translate the article into your language.

Newspaper sales are dropping. Even the ten big national newspapers with a combined circulation of over 11,000,000 are beginning to lose readers. The main reason for this is online papers. Some people prefer to switch on their computers and read articles and features when they want to. And what would happen if newspapers finally disappeared? We'd spend even more time in front of a screen.

_____

_____

_____

_____

_____

_____

_____

_____

8B | Protests

UNREAL CONDITIONS (TYPE 2)

1 Complete the sentences in column A with the phrases in column B to make conditional sentences.

A

1 The mobile phone market would grow

2 Morrison had always claimed that if he won,

3 A recent report suggests that up to 25% more young people would buy property

4 If oil prices stopped rising,

5 If electronic sensors were put on goalposts,

6 The government claimed that the new vaccine would save almost a million lives a year

B

a if the price of phones went down.

b we would probably see a global economic recovery.

c he'd give half of the money to charity and he kept his promise.

d if it was introduced into schools across the country.

e the Football Referee Association say their members would feel happier.

f if housing wasn't so expensive.

2 Rewrite the sentences from newspapers as conditional sentences.

1 The government is not so popular now because they don't listen to people.
The government *would be more popular if they listened to people.*

2 There is no cure for AIDS yet. As a result, three million people die every year.
If a cure for AIDS was found, _____
_____.

3 Turning down heating by 1°C in winter saves up to 10% off people's heating bills.
People would _____
_____.

4 20% of British adults don't eat well enough or exercise enough. Because of that they are extremely fat.
_____, 20% of British adults wouldn't be fat.

3 Find and correct the six mistakes in the text.

> Try to imagine a world where suddenly we didn't have any news. No radio, TV, newspapers or online papers. What did that be like? We would all be cut off from the rest of the world. All the structures that support our life will collapse, from governments to supermarkets to transport systems and hospitals. It was like a terrible dream. We would have to live in small communities to protect ourselves from each other. And how would we keep warm? Where would we find food? It won't be a happy world. If such a thing would happen, it would be like moving back in time to the dark ages. I don't want to live in such a world.

DICTATION

4 🔊 **30** Write the text that you hear.

_____
_____
_____
_____
_____

40

8c | Bank robbers

UNREAL CONDITIONS (TYPE 3)

1 Read the story about two motorcyclists. Then rearrange the phrases to make conditional sentences.

Bikers blow small fortune on motorway

Two unhappy motorcyclists on their way to buy a car lost £10,500 in cash when the bag one of them was carrying split open. The unlucky bikers pulled off the road and tried to collect as much of it as they could, but most of it flew across the motorway. They were soon joined by motorists who had pulled over to help. However, it was too windy and the motorway was too busy to be able to save more than £500 of the original £11,000.

To make a terrible situation worse, the poor motorcyclists broke down further along the motorway. Their day was further complicated when the police became interested in the story. A spokeswoman for the police said, 'The fact they had that much money on them did cause suspicion.' It soon became clear, however, that the poor bikers were telling the truth. They probably wished they had taken the train.

1 wouldn't have   the bag hadn't   if   any
  money   split open, they   lost .

_____

2 a busy motorway,   have lost so much money
  hadn't happened on   if the accident   they wouldn't .

_____

3 stopped to   have rescued even less money   people
  hadn't   help them, they would   if some .

_____

4 been £10,500 richer   taken a cheque   they would
  have   instead of cash   if they had .

_____

5 never have   money in cash on them   the police
  would   if they hadn't had so much   been suspicious .

_____

6 if they   by train, they   have lost a penny   had
  travelled   wouldn't .

_____

2 Rewrite the sentences to make past conditional sentences.

1 The robber didn't order coffee, so the clerk wasn't able to open the cash till.
  If the robber had ordered coffee, *the clerk would have been able to open the cash till.*

2 Because the thief left evidence, he was arrested by the police.
  If the thief hadn't left _____.

3 A burglar called his mother from his victim's house. As a result, the police were able to catch the burglar.
  The police wouldn't have caught _____.

LAW & ORDER

3 Complete the text with words and phrases from the box.

judge	robber	evidence	robbery	guilty
arrested	trial	sentenced		

A man walked into a fast-food restaurant in Michigan in the US, pulled out a gun and said to the clerk, 'This is a stick-up! Give me all your cash.' The clerk apologized and said he couldn't open the cash till without a food order. When the man ordered onion rings, the clerk said they weren't available for breakfast. The frustrated (1) _____ walked away and left a lot of (2) _____. He was caught on CCTV and also left his gun on the counter covered in fingerprints. He was (3) _____ two hours later and charged with attempted (4) _____ and carrying a gun. After a three-minute (5) _____, the (6) _____ found him (7) _____ and (8) _____ him to six months in jail.

READ & LISTEN

4 **31** Read and listen to the reading text on page 81 of the Student's Book.

8D | Driving

Offers

1 Rearrange the words to make offers in the dialogue.

Arnold: Hi, Bill. Hey, what's the matter?

(1) you   something   I do   can   for ?

_____

Bill: No, no it's OK, thanks. I just have to write this assignment for tomorrow.

Arnold: Uh-huh. (2) you a hand   like   I'll give if you ._____ .

Bill: No, I'll manage, thanks.

Arnold: Oh, come on Bill. (3) you   me   help   let

_____ … that's what friends are for.

Bill: Well, OK. Great, thanks a lot.

Arnold: (4) like me   to do   you   would   what ?

_____

Bill: Well, I've written my assignment, but all by hand. I just need to type it up so …

Arnold: OK, no problem. (5) it up for   me to   do you want   type   you _____

_____

Bill: Oh, yes! Thanks! That's really kind of you. But there are 40 pages.

Arnold: Four zero!? (6) I   shall   now   start ?

_____

2 Choose the best answer a, b or c.

1 I'm going to the shops. Can I get you anything?
   a) No, thanks. I'll manage. b) Would you like some help? c) That's really kind of you.

2 Do you want me to give you a lift to the station? I'd be happy to.
   a) That would be lovely. b) Yes. I'll manage, thanks.
   c) No!

3 Shall I lend you £5? I've got lots of cash on me.
   a) Would you like some change? b) No, it's OK, thanks.
   c) Yes.

4 Would you like me to have a look at your computer? Perhaps I can fix it.
   a) That's really kind of you. b) No, that would be great.
   c) Can you help me?

5 Can I give you a hand with those bags? They look heavy.
   a) No! b) Can I do anything for you?
   c) No, I'll manage, thank you.

Compound nouns (driving)

3 Complete the story with compound nouns from the box.

| traffic light | one-way street | driving licence |
| motorway | no-parking zone | speed limit |

Mr Reginald Burton says he is one of the worst drivers in Britain and it seems a judge agrees with him. The 89-year-old driver has now lost his (1) _____ for eleven years as a result of a number of driving offences committed over the last seven months. He explained to our reporter, 'On one occasion I was driving up a road and only realized it was a (2) _____ when I met a police car coming the other way.' Another time he was stopped by the police for driving 50 miles over the (3) _____ on the M4 (4) _____ .

'My last and final offence happened just three weeks ago. The police pulled me over for driving through a (5) _____ when it was red.'

Mrs Burton was happy about the verdict. 'It will save us a lot of money. My husband gets a parking ticket at least once a month for leaving the car in a (6) _____ .'

🔘 Dictation

4 🔘 **32** Write the short dialogues that you hear.

1 A: _____ .

   B: _____ .

2 A: _____ ?

   B: _____ .

3 A: _____ ?

   B: _____ .

4 A: _____ ?

   B: _____ .

8 | Reading

THE FUTURE OF THE PRESS?

1 Interesting things are happening in the press. Newspaper circulation in Europe is falling and Ireland and the UK have experienced the biggest drop. Despite this, the news isn't all bad for the industry. Global newspaper sales are increasing and revenue from ads is still very strong. Nevertheless, it is clear that newspapers need to change to meet the demands of a rapidly changing readership in a digital world.

2 The industry in Europe has made a number of changes, such as introducing more colour and moving from the big, bulky broadsheets to the much more user-friendly tabloid size. The most radical innovation has been the introduction of online newspapers, which have boomed since their introduction a little over ten years ago. But are online papers here to stay? On the one hand, it is clear from the massive increase in online readers that e-papers are popular. On the other hand, their financial future is not so certain. This is basically because most people are not prepared to pay for online news. In fact, if it wasn't for advertising, online newspapers would have a very hard time indeed.

3 A growing number of people are reading electronic newspapers instead of the print press and with good reason. First of all, they can read the news whenever they want. Secondly, readers are free to explore a subject as much or as little as they want. Thirdly, it is the perfect medium for 'real-time' news. Take, for example, the Olympic® Games in Athens in 2004. Readers were able to get minute-by-minute coverage at any hour of the day. Only 24-hour news on TV could compete with that. Arguably the biggest attraction is that this news is absolutely free, at least for now. It's no great surprise that online news is thriving. Publishers, editors and journalists are all talking about what this will mean for the future.

4 The general view is that the future 'paper' will be a multimedia mix. Advanced technology and programming software will allow the user to create their own 'news package'. And it will arrive instantaneously, fed by super-fast internet connections. The reader will receive up-to-the-minute news about everything from their local traffic problems to updates on news of specific interest to them. Nobody knows for sure what will happen, but as one expert put it, 'We won't be saying "Here is the news", we will be saying, "Here is your news."'

1 Read the article and match the headings a–d to the paragraphs 1–4.

☐ a Why readers like e-papers
☐ b Newspaper sales
☐ c How news will change
☐ d Online papers here to stay?

2 Read the summaries of each paragraph and correct one mistake in each summary.

Paragraph 1
Newspaper sales are rising all over the world. As a result, newspapers do things differently to keep their readers.

Paragraph 2
The newspaper industry has made a number of changes, one of which is the creation of online newspapers. These have become very popular and they have made money through advertising and people paying to read them.

Paragraph 3
There are a few reasons why people like e-newspapers. They're free, you can read as much as you want, when you want and they're available twelve hours a day.

Paragraph 4
In the future, the news will arrive if it happens. It will be a combination of different media. The reader will buy packages of news which are created especially for them.

3 Find words or phrases in the article which mean the same as the definitions 1–5. The paragraph numbers are in brackets.

1 income from business activities (1)
2 newspapers that are printed on very large pages (2)
3 news that is reported as soon as it happens (3)
4 becoming very successful (3)
5 report or broadcast that contains the most recent information (4)

READ & LISTEN

4 🔘 33 Listen to Reading 8 *The future of the press?* on the CD and read the article again.

9A | The shopping basket

ARTICLES & DETERMINERS

1 Choose the correct articles to complete the text.

Today I'm having (1) *a / the* picnic. I'm going to get most of (2) *some / the* food at my local delicatessen – (3) *some / the* deli in Dorset Road. Now I need (4) *any / some* good bread and (5) *a / some* cheese, too. I also want to pick up some Greek olives, but they don't have (6) *some / any* at the Italian deli. I'll need to get them later. Now what else? Bread, cheese, olives … oh and salad. I'll get (7) *the / any* salad later when I buy (8) *a / the* olives.

2 Complete the newspaper article with *a, the, –* (no word), *some* or *any*.

(1) _____ number of obese children in the UK has tripled in the past 20 years, with the result that one in ten six-year-olds and one in six fifteen-year-olds are now seriously overweight. Too many children are eating (2) _____ food that is high in salt, sugar and fat. (3) _____ children are not eating (4) _____ vegetables at all and only a little fruit.

Mintel, a market research company has just published (5) _____ report on the problem. A senior market analyst at Mintel, Maria Elustondo, said, 'There is obviously a strong carbohydrate element to children's diet these days, with (6) _____ bread, fruit, biscuits, cereals and tomato ketchup named as the top five foods for Britain's seven to sixteen-year-old children.'

Mintel's research also showed that of the five most popular 'between meals' food, only one option, fruit, was healthy. The other four (crisps, chocolate, sweets and biscuits), were high in (7) _____ sugar, fat and salt.

The research also pointed out that food was not the only problem. Too many children spend too much time in front of the TV or computer and don't get (8) _____ exercise. They need to get out and do some physical exercise.

CONTAINERS

3 Complete the phrases 1–8 with as many nouns as possible from the box.

ice cream	beer	biscuits	tomato soup
dog food	crackers	crisps	coffee
free-range eggs	whisky	strawberry jam	
margarine	milk	mineral water	olive oil
peanuts	tissues	tuna	

1 a tub of
2 a jar of
3 a bottle of
4 a packet of

5 a tin of
6 a box of
7 a can of
8 a carton of

4 Complete the dialogue with containers from exercise 6.

Dulcie: Can you get a (1) _____ of coffee and a (2) _____ of biscuits when you go to the supermarket?

Jane: Sure. I'll get a (3) _____ of cat food for the cat, too.

Dulcie: Yes. Good idea. I'm cooking dinner and I need a (4) _____ of eggs and a (5) _____ of olive oil. Can you get them for me?

Jane: Of course. I'll do dessert. I'll get some strawberries and a (6) _____ of cream. Oh, and a (7) _____ of ice cream, too. I love ice cream!

🌐 DICTATION

5 🌐 **34** Write the dialogue that you hear.

_____

_____

_____

_____

_____

_____

🌐 READ & LISTEN

6 🌐 **35** Read and listen to the reading text *Checking out the check out* on page 87 of the Student's Book.

9B | Shoppers

QUANTIFIERS 1

1 Choose the best determiners to complete the article.

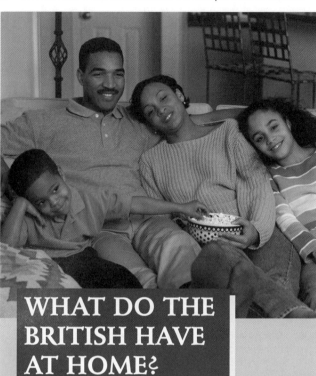

WHAT DO THE BRITISH HAVE AT HOME?

The Office for National Statistics (ONS) produces information about Britain. Their last 'General Household Survey' looked at the 'consumer durables' that British own.

According to the most recent survey, (1) *all / most* households had at least one TV (99%) and one washing machine (96%). (2) *Some / Many* of them also had a computer at home (76%) and just under half had a car (45%). Interestingly, (3) *most / none* people still have a fixed telephone in their homes (91%), but that number was beginning to gradually fall as (4) *most / some* people now own and prefer to use a mobile phone (84%).

The ownership of CD players is still very high. Almost (5) *many / all* of the people in Britain have one. That figure will inevitably change as new technology replaces both CD players and DVD players. In fact, (6) *any / most* researchers are predicting that (7) *none / any* of Britain's households will have CD players within the next ten years. Indeed, many people are predicting that there won't be (8) *some / any* DVDs or CDs at all in the not-so-distant future because we will download everything we want to watch or listen to from the internet.

SHOPPING

2 Complete the dialogue with words or phrases from the box.

> shop assistant   shopping centre/mall   shopaholic
> window shopping   shoplifters   security guard
> online shopping   high street shopping

Andrea: Hi, Claire. Want to come shopping? They've just opened a few new shops in the (1) _____.

Claire: Yeah, I know. Do you know that Carrie has got a job as a (2) _____ in a perfume shop there, selling that new French brand?

Andrea: Has she? My brother's going to work there, too.

Claire: Really! Work in a perfume shop, too?

Andrea: No way, he's far too macho. He's going to be a (3) _____.

Claire: What!? Catching all the (4) _____ who walk off with CDs up their jumpers?

Andrea: Yep, that's the idea. Anyway, want to shop?

Claire: I don't have any money, but we could go (5) _____.

Andrea: Absolutely. I haven't got much money either. Shall we ask Luisa?

Claire: No. She told me that she never wants to go (6) _____ again.

Andrea: What!? Luisa stop shopping! Impossible!! She's a (7) _____!!!

Claire: I know. She said she would prefer to shop from the comfort of her bedroom. She's only interested in (8) _____ now!

TRANSLATION

3 Translate the sentences into your language.

1 None of the 60–75 age group had bought any clothing on the internet.

_____.

2 Most online shoppers buy books, music and holidays.

_____.

3 Most shoppers prefer to go to the big supermarkets on the outskirts of town.

_____.

4 High street shopping may become a thing of the past as more people shop online.

_____.

5 Massive supermarkets are slowly killing off small stores and corner shops.

_____.

9c | E-shopping

COLLOCATIONS WITH TAKE

1 Complete the advert with words or phrases from the box.

> a little time   advice   breath away
> a look at   our word   advantage of

Click4clothes

for prices you can't resist

Now you're here, take (1) _____ to look around the store. These unbelievable prices will take your (2) _____: pure cotton T-shirts down to £3.99. Take (3) _____ these jeans – just £7.99. Take (4) _____ a further 10% off these prices with your first online order. You won't find such good quality at these prices anywhere online. But don't just take (5) _____ for it. Look around and if you can find the same thing cheaper online, we'll refund you your money. So take our (6) _____ and buy now. You won't be sorry.

QUANTIFIERS 2

2 Choose the best quantifiers to complete the text.

Too (1) *many / much* people are still worried about shopping online according to a new survey. Although security on the net has improved enormously, (2) *not many / plenty* of people are still worried about giving out personal information. (3) *Not many / A lot of* the people interviewed felt that the government did (4) *little / a little* to fight credit card fraud. The reality is actually the opposite. Secure payment systems mean that only (5) *a few / too many* people have had credit card problems – just 1% in fact. Another common concern that e-shoppers have is that they can't touch or see what they want to buy. 'Five years ago very (6) *little / few* was done to help customers with these worries,' said Kathy Corman, visual director of SeeFeelBuy. 'But technology is moving fast. There are even (7) *few / a few* sites that have personalized virtual dressing rooms. It won't be long before you'll be able to see yourself dancing in that new dress.'

3 Do this quiz on net addiction to see if you have a problem. When you have finished, tick the answers you think a netaholic would give.

Are you a netaholic?

1 How much time do you spend on the internet?
a) none at all ☐
b) not much ☐
c) a normal amount ☐
d) a lot ☐ e) too much ☐

2 How many things have you bought online?
a) none ☐ b) a few things ☐ c) some things ☐
d) plenty of stuff ☐ e) too many things ☐

3 How many friends have you got?
a) very few ☐ b) a few ☐ c) enough ☐
d) plenty ☐ e) too many ☐

4 How much time do you spend going out and seeing friends?
a) very little ☐ b) a little ☐ c) enough ☐
d) plenty ☐ e) too much ☐

5 Do your friends ever complain about how much time you spend on the internet?
a) yes, all the time ☐ b) often, but that's OK ☐
c) sometimes ☐ d) a little ☐ e) never ☐

6 How many times have you found it difficult to go offline?
a) never ☐ b) not many ☐ c) sometimes ☐
d) loads of times ☐ e) too many times to count ☐

[Submit your answers]

DICTATION

4 🔊 **36** Write the text that you hear.

_____

_____

_____

_____

_____

9D | Phone calls

COMPLAINTS

1 Rearrange what the customer (C) says to the shop assistant (SA) to complete the dialogue.

C: wrong with this think
there's laptop I something .
(1) _____

SA: I see. What seems to be the problem, sir?

C: well, and I'm speakers it yesterday
with the I only bought having problems .
(2) _____

SA: I'm terribly sorry, sir. How can I help? Are the speakers too quiet?

C: just no , work they don't .
(3) _____

SA: Well, we can send the laptop back to the manufacturers, if you like.

C: but want money I to my back have .
(4) _____

SA: I'm afraid we can't do that.

C: is unacceptable I'm but sorry, this .
(5) _____

SA: I'm sure they'll sort out the problem if we send it back.

C: I speak the could to please ? manager , .
(6) _____

SA: I'm afraid she's on holiday. Please fill in this form and I'll send the laptop to …

VOCABULARY FROM THE LESSON

2 Complete the verbs 1–8 with the phrases a–h.

1	have	a	the matter
2	be	b	a look
3	send	c	in touch
4	keep	d	a text
5	make	e	someone through
6	get	f	a complaint
7	be	g	something repaired
8	put	h	busy

PREPOSITIONAL PHRASES

3 Complete the sentences with prepositions from the box.

> by   in   in   by   on   in   in   in

1 Could you look through the form ____ detail, please?
2 We were ____ a hurry because we were late for the concert.
3 Please write your name ____ full.
4 Have you ever been ____ trouble at work?
5 ____ average, I send about 20 texts a day.
6 I called him David ____ mistake!
7 Were you ____ class when the alarm went off?
8 I learnt the poem ____ heart.

4 Match the sentences and questions 1–8 in exercise 3 to the responses a–h.

- [ ] a Yes, we were. We had to go outside, but it was a false alarm.
- [ ] b Sure. There are a lot of sections to fill in, aren't there?
- [ ] c Yes, once. My boss caught me phoning my girlfriend in Brazil.
- [ ] d Oh, no. Wasn't that your last boyfriend's name?
- [ ] e Did you get there in time in the end?
- [ ] f Wow! That's a lot. I hardly ever send any.
- [ ] g OK. Should I include my middle name?
- [ ] h Really? OK. Let's hear it.

TRANSLATION

5 Translate the dialogue into your language.

A: Could I speak to the manager, please?
B: That's me. How can I help?
A: I recently bought this mobile phone.
B: I see. And what seems to be the problem, madam?
A: I'm having problems turning it on.
B: Oh, right. Well, see this little button here?
A: This one?
B: Yes, try pushing it down.
A: Oh, look. It's come on! How pretty! Thank you so much.

_____

_____

_____

_____

_____

_____

1 Read the article and match the headings a–c to the paragraphs 1–3.

a The largest mall
b The most richly-decorated mall
c The most historical mall

THE WORLD'S GREATEST SHOPPING MALLS

Whether you love shopping or hate it, visiting some of the world's greatest shopping malls can be an exciting experience. Many of them feature truly amazing pieces of architecture, ranging from monumental sculptures designed by internationally-renowned artists to fantastic versions of famous buildings from around the world. Some of them are so huge that they have more shops than many towns. And all of them, of course, offer a bewildering array of shops and brands. Here are some of our favourites …

1 _____
The scorching heat of countries in the Middle East means that air-conditioned, indoor shopping malls are not just popular but absolutely essential there. And one of the most beautiful and opulent is Villagio in Doha. The ceiling is painted to look like the sky, and the huge white marble hall, which is filled with pillars and bridges, looks more like a palace than the interior of a mall. And if you are a fan of upmarket designer fashions, you'll find most of the top labels and designers here.

2 _____
In the last twenty years, a growing, wealthy middle class and a huge demand for luxury goods in countries like Russia and China has resulted in a boom in the development of shopping malls. And one iconic place that has benefitted from this growth is GUM on Red Square in Moscow. When Russia was a communist country, GUM was the showcase of its socialist economy. It was the largest and most important shop in the country in those days. Since the introduction of capitalism, the shop has been transformed. It is now full of luxury brands. However, it still retains the style and grandeur of its original late nineteenth century design, and many go there to admire the architecture rather than check out the labels.

3 _____
The New South China Mall does not have many of the world's leading brands, and it doesn't have the style or opulence of Villagio or GUM, but one thing it does have is sheer size. It's hard to say which mall is bigger than all the others, but, in one regard, this mall can claim this prize. It has more shopping space than any other mall in the world. Indeed, there is space in the mall for almost 2,500 shops.

The place is divided into seven different sections, all of which are modelled on different regions of the world. In the section based on Paris, you can see a replica of the Arc de Triomphe, and in the Venice section there is a canal with gondolas which is over two kilometres long.

2 Read the article again and choose the best answer, a or b.

1 Visiting a great shopping mall can be exciting because of …
   a) the original buildings.   b) the original sculptures.
2 Shopping malls in the Middle East are essential because …
   a) they have the best shops.
   b) it's too hot to shop outside.
3 The décor at Villagio in Doha makes you feel like you are …
   a) in a village.   b) outdoors.
4 The shops at Villagio are …
   a) expensive and select.   b) economical and popular.
5 GUM has always …
   a) had luxurious shops.   b) had an iconic status.
6 The New South China Mall is …
   a) massive.   b) opulent.

3 Find words or phrases in the article which mean the same as the definitions 1–9 below. The paragraph numbers are in brackets.

1 famous around the world (1)
2 very big (1)
3 confusing selection (1)
4 very hot (2)
5 very important (2)
6 very rich and luxurious (2)
7 a period of fast economic growth (3)
8 changed completely (3)
9 extreme (size) (4)

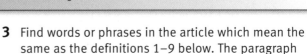

READ & LISTEN

4 **37** Listen to Reading 9 *The world's greatest shopping malls* on the CD and read the article again.

10A | Secrets

MODALS OF SPECULATION 1 (PRESENT TIME)

1 Imagine that you find the objects in the pictures below in a handbag. Write sentences about the owner of the bag using the information and the modals.

1	TARJETA DE IDENTIFICACIÓN COSTA RICA	Costa Rican (*must*)
2	Learn French	French (*can't*)
3		divorced (*could*)
4		children (*might*)
5		smoke (*may*)
6	Chopin's Piano	piano (*might*)
7	JULIA LOPEZ 47 HASELMERE ROAD BIRMINGHAM TOTAL CALLS 78 SAVER CALLS 32 02488 121556 21/04 0.025 542111 587126 22/04 1.258 047891 0222 27/04 8.256	Birmingham (*must*)

1 *She must be Costa Rican.*
2 _____ .
3 _____ .
4 _____ .
5 _____ .
6 _____ .
7 _____ .

ILLUSIONS

2 Complete the text with words from the box.

audiences	tricks	perform	magician
vanish	magical	pretending	fake

The American illusionist, David Blaine must be the most famous living (1) _____.
He used to (2) _____ card tricks in bars in New York, but Blaine wanted more. In 1997, he walked into the boardroom of ABC television and got a million-dollar contract by doing an unbelievable card trick and then levitating his body two feet off the floor. The contract led to a one-hour TV show called *David Blaine: Street Magic*. (3) _____ all over the world watched him do incredible (4) _____ such as making cards (5) _____ and then reappear in a shop window. In 2003, he was in London, living in a transparent plastic box up in the air for 45 days. He said that he had nothing but water to keep him alive. Some thought that he was (6) _____ and that the water actually contained food of some sort. Whether you think it's all real or completely (7) _____, there's no escaping the fact that Blaine is (8) _____ to watch.

🔊 DICTATION

3 🔊 **38** Write the dialogue that you hear.

_____
_____
_____
_____
_____
_____
_____
_____

10B | Fact or fiction?

WORD FAMILIES

1 Complete the opinions with the best word.

1 There's a strong *likelihood / unlikely / likely* that a small group of people control most of the world.
2 It is a *probability / probably / improbable* that the secret services listen to everything we say.
3 It's absolutely *possibility / impossible / impossibility* for aliens to be living amongst us.
4 The result of the election is an absolute *certainty / certain / uncertain*.
5 There is a small *impossible / possibility / impossibility* that the HIV virus was developed as a secret weapon.

2 Complete the text with the correct form of the words in brackets.

The (1) _____ (*likely*) that people from another planet colonized Earth thousands of years ago seems (2) _____ (*probable*). However, some people (3) _____ (*definite*) think it's true. They believe that an alien race brought their culture and technology from another planet and passed it on to the primitive people on Earth at that time. They argue that building the pyramids, for example, would have been (4) _____ (*possible*) if they hadn't visited us. It's (5) _____ (*certain*) where this idea first came from. It was (6) _____ (*probable*) invented by someone on the internet. However, the (7) _____ (*possible*) that our culture came from another planet is (8) _____ (*certain*) something to think about. Personally, however, I think that the (9) _____ (*probable*) of this happening is so low – so (10) _____ (*likely*) – that I don't think I'll be thinking about it for very long!

MODALS OF SPECULATION 2 (PRESENT TIME)

3 Choose the best response, a, b or c.

1 Your unhappy friend phones you from a bus stop and asks you for a lift. There's been no bus for 40 minutes and it's snowing.
   a) She could be waiting.
   b) She must be freezing.
   c) She could be having fun.
2 An old school friend says they heard your old friend Zac is working as a ski instructor. That's not possible because you know that Zac can't ski.
   a) Zac couldn't be working as a ski instructor.
   b) My old school friend can't be lying.
   c) Zac must be working as a ski instructor.
3 You are waiting for your friend in an Indian restaurant called *The Sitar*. Unfortunately, there are two *Sitars* in town. There's a small possibility he's at the other one.
   a) He must be having dinner at home.
   b) He can't be having dinner at the other restaurant.
   c) He could be waiting for me at the other restaurant.
4 Your friend Amelia is on a beach holiday in Greece and it's 11am there. You know she loves getting up at 9am to go sunbathing.
   a) She might be dancing in a club.
   b) She must be sunbathing.
   c) She could be sleeping in bed.

TRANSLATION

4 Translate the text into your language.

Interpol, the international police organization, is looking for the international bank robber, Johnny Raffles. Raffles has probably robbed 26 banks in eighteen different countries and has been called the *Magic Magician*. As a result of his success, he must be making more money than any head of government in the world. Interpol believe that he could be living in Germany or America. The likelihood of catching this brilliant thief is small, but Interpol never give up.

_____

_____

_____

_____

_____

_____

10c | Mysteries

MODALS OF SPECULATION (PAST TIME)

1 Complete the text with phrases from the box.

> could they have been used
> might have been   must have been drawn
> could the Nazca people have managed
> must have been   could have had

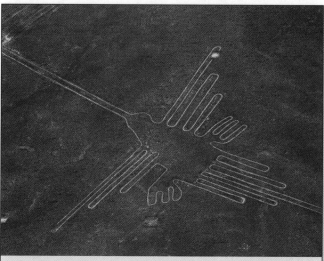

The Nazca lines are gigantic drawings of geometric shapes, animals, spiders and fish drawn by the Nazca people in the Peruvian desert. Scientists believe they (1) _____ over 2,000 years ago. One of the most amazing things about these pictures is that they can only be seen from the air, so how (2) _____ to draw such enormous pictures?

Various theories have been put forward. Erich von Däniken was positive that they (3) _____ the work of a superior race of aliens from another planet. He thought the lines made an airfield for alien spaceships. How (4) _____ as an airfield? Firstly, the lines would have been too confusing and secondly, if aliens had landed there, why were there no marks left by their spacecraft? Other theories suggest that the lines (5) _____ for foot races, for irrigation or for astronomical purposes. But none of these could really explain the lines. More probable theories have been made since then. Perhaps the lines (6) _____ a religious purpose; a place created by the Nazca for their gods. Yet nobody has ever explained the Nazca lines and they remain a wonderful mystery.

VERBS FOLLOWED BY INFINITIVE

2 Choose the best phrases to complete the dialogue.

Karen: Did you see that programme about the Russian girl, Natasha Demkina who (1) *refused to / claimed to* be able to see people's illnesses?

Balvir: You're joking?

Karen: No. She found she had a special talent and (2) *tried to / deserved to* help dozens of people in her home town.

Balvir: And was she a fake?

Karen: Who knows? Some scientists thought she (3) *deserved to / refused to* be taken seriously.

Balvir: So did she have to do tests and stuff?

Karen: They did some scientific tests and she (4) *seemed to / deserved to* work out what was wrong with several patients.

Balvir: Wow! So she must have special powers.

Karen: Well, the scientists couldn't agree on that. Some (5) *deserved to / began to* accept that she was special and thought she (6) *managed to / refused to* see these things.

🔘 DICTATION

3 🔘 **39** Write the dialogue that you hear.

_____

_____

_____

_____

_____

_____

10D | Strictly confidential

ADVANTAGES & DISADVANTAGES

1 Decide if the meaning of each of the following words or phrases is positive (P) or negative (N).

1 drawback   __
2 benefit   __
3 problem   __
4 advantage   __
5 pro   __
6 trouble   __
7 con   __
8 no point in __

2 Choose the best options to complete the arguments in the leaflet

DRUG TESTING IN SCHOOLS

The British government is thinking about introducing random drug testing in schools.
Here are some of the main arguments for and against the idea. What do you think?

A major advantage of drug (1) *test / testing* is that students are less likely to take drugs if they think they may be caught.

There are many (2) *benefits / drawbacks* to drug testing, like giving the schools another option in fighting the war on drug abuse.

The (3) *benefit / disadvantage* of drug testing is that it's very expensive to do properly.

The (4) *trouble / con* is it's undemocratic. If a school has a problem with drugs, they should work with the students who have a problem, not assume the whole school is guilty.

The (5) *con / problem* with drug testing by individual schools is that there will be chaos. If the government is serious, they need to have one system for the whole country.

The (6) *advantage / pro* of drug testing is that it gives students an excuse to say 'no' when they are under pressure from their friends to take drugs.

IDIOMS

3 Complete the sentences with idioms from the box.

| bright and early | cracking | high point |
| dragging your feet | it safe | to the point |

1 Come on, you lot! If you don't get _____, we'll miss the plane.
2 And my team won the cup! It was the happiest moment of my life. Well, maybe not, but it was the _____ of my year.
3 He was going on and on about unimportant little things and not saying what he really wanted to. So I lost my patience and told him to get _____.
4 I'm like my dad. He never liked to take risks and I always prefer to play _____, too.
5 This report has to be finished today, so stop _____ and just do it!
6 I prefer to get up _____ because I work best in the morning.

TRANSLATION

4 Translate the dialogue into your language.

A: The good thing about getting up bright and early is that you feel you are really using the day.
B: Not for me. I feel sleepy in the morning.
A: Maybe. But the drawback of late nights is that you can't get cracking in the morning.
B: Yeah, yeah. OK, I know there are pros and cons, but this conversation is too serious for seven in the morning. Where's the coffee?

_____

_____

_____

_____

_____

_____

_____

'Lucky' Lord Lucan – ALIVE OR DEAD?

ON NOVEMBER 8 1974 Lord Lucan, a British aristocrat, vanished. The day before, his children's nanny had been brutally murdered and his wife had been attacked, too. To this day the British public are still interested in the murder case because Lucan has never been found. Now, over 30 years later, the police have reopened the case, hoping that new DNA techniques will help solve this murder mystery.

People suspected that 'Lucky', as he was called by friends, wanted to kill his wife he no longer lived with. They say that Lucan entered his old house and, in the dark, killed the nanny by mistake. His estranged wife heard noises, came downstairs and was also attacked, but managed to escape. Seven months after the murder, a jury concluded that Lucan had killed the nanny.

What happened next is unclear, but there are several theories which fall into one of three categories: he may have killed himself, he could have escaped or he might have been killed. It appears that the night after the murder, 'Lucky' borrowed a car and drove it to the English coast. In 2000, John Aspinall, a close friend of Lucan's, said in an interview that he thought Lucan had committed suicide by sinking his boat in the English Channel.

Another version of events says that 'Lucky' left the blood-soaked car on the coast and took a ferry to France. He was met there by someone who drove him to safety in another country. However, after a time, his rescuers became worried that they would become involved in the murder, too and so Lucan was killed.

A further fascinating theory was made in the book *Dead Lucky* by Duncan MacLaughlin, a former detective. He believes that Lucan travelled to Goa, India, where he assumed the identity of a Mr Barry Haplin. Lucan then lived in Goa till his death in 1996. In the end the claim turned out to be a case of mistaken identity. The man who died in 1996 was really Haplin, an ex-schoolteacher turned hippy. So what is the truth about 'Lucky'? DNA testing has solved many murder cases, but who knows if it can close the book on this one.

---

1 Read the article. Choose the best ending a, b or c.

1 The public are still interested in the investigation because …
   a) of the terrible murder.
   b) of the use of new DNA techniques.
   c) Lord Lucan has never been found.

2 It is thought that Lucan killed the nanny because …
   a) she was looking after the children.
   b) she was a friend of Lucan's.
   c) it was dark and he thought she was Lady Lucan.

3 Aspinall thought Lucan killed himself by …
   a) jumping into water.   b) sailing his boat.
   c) sinking his boat.

4 Lucan could have been killed because people …
   a) didn't want the police to catch him.
   b) thought he might talk to the police about them if he was caught.
   c) were unhappy with him.

5 Ex-detective MacLaughlin claimed that Barry Haplin …
   a) was an old schoolteacher.
   b) died in Goa, India.
   c) was really Lord Lucan in disguise.

2 Read the summary of the article and correct the six factual mistakes in it.

In 1974, Lord Lucan vanished two days after his wife was horribly murdered. Lucan has never been seen since. New DNA techniques mean the police have solved the case and they have reopened it.

People said that 'Lucky' wanted to kill his wife. Unfortunately he killed his nanny by mistake. Seven months later he was accused of the murder.

There are two theories about what happened to him. A close friend said that he sank his own boat off the English coast to kill himself. Another story says someone helped him by meeting him and driving him to France, but later murdered him. A book was written describing another theory that Lucan travelled to India where he became Mr Barry Haplin and lived in Goa until he died in 1996. This theory was wrong though. Haplin was not Lucan – he was a detective.

🔊 READ & LISTEN

3 🔊 **40** Listen to Reading 10 *'Lucky' Lord Lucan – alive or dead?* on the CD and read the article again.

11A | Total sport

PASSIVE

1 Choose the correct verb forms to complete the text.

File Edit View Favourites Tools Help Links ➤

THE ORIGINS OF
Taekwondo

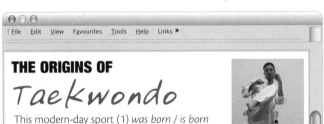

This modern-day sport (1) *was born / is born* from an ancient martial art. Records show that it (2) *was being practised / is being practised* as early as 50 BC in Silla, one of three kingdoms in pre-Korean history. Because Silla (3) *was always attacked / was always being attacked* by Japanese pirates, an early form of the art was taught to soldiers. As a result, the Kingdom (4) *had to be / could be* protected. Schools (5) *was founded / were founded* to train these Hwarang or 'warriors'. They became travellers and taught their art to the ordinary people.

The martial art went through numerous changes over the next thousand plus years and almost disappeared during Japan's invasion of Korea from 1909 until 1945. However, after Korea's independence in 1945, new Kwans or martial arts schools (6) *was opened / were opened*. Ten years later, a group of Korean martial arts leaders gave this art one name, Tae Kwon Do. 'Tae' means kick; 'Kwon' means strike and 'Do' means method or way. Tae Kwon Do, the 'art of kicking and striking', became the Korean martial art. The sport has a strict code and violence (7) *was not allowed / is not allowed*. In 1973, the World Taekwondo Federation (8) *has been established / was established* and recognized by the Korean government.

---

2 Complete the text with the verbs in brackets in the passive.

SPORTS QUIZ

Sport 1 _____

This sport (1) _____ (*write*) about in ancient Greek, Roman, Persian, Indian and Chinese history. It (2) _____ (*practise*) in Greece where it was mainly used to prepare young men to fight in wars, and it (3) _____ (*include*) in the Olympic® Games in 688 BC. The men's hands (4) _____ (*cover*) with leather bands to protect them at that time. The sport as we know it (5) _____ (*revive*) in 18ᵗʰ century England and (6) _____ (*practise*) in its present form since the 1880s, with the two men in a small, square space and the audience seated all around them. Nowadays, it (7) _____ (*also / promote*) as a sport for women, both as participants and spectators.

Sport 2 _____

This sport developed out of parachuting in the 1960s. At the time special holes (8) _____ (*cut*) in a parachute to slow the fall and to allow the pilot to direct the parachute. Later, by changing the design, the parachute (9) _____ (*pull*) up into the air by a small plane. But one more development (10) _____ (*need*) – a square sail. Once this (11) _____ (*develop*), the sport was ready to take off. That happened in the French town of Mieussy where pilots managed to fly into the air by running down the hillsides of the Alps. Since then, this sport (12) _____ (*be*) very popular in Ölü Deniz, in Turkey. As you read this, hundreds of these 'birds' (13) _____ (*fly*) all over the world.

Now complete the headings with the sports.

SPORT

3 Match the descriptions 1–5 to sports from the box.

| rugby   athletics   baseball   water polo   boxing |

1 This involves a number of different sports like the 100 metres and the high jump. _____
2 In this team game, you have to hit a ball with a wooden bat and then run around four 'bases'. If you succeed, you score a 'run'. _____
3 This is a very skilful sport, but many people think it just consists of two people hitting each other. _____
4 The aim is to run with the ball in your arms, pass it and kick it. The objective is to score 'a try'. _____
5 There are seven players, one of which is a goalkeeper. The match is played in water. _____

🔊 DICTATION

4 🔊 **41** Write the text that you hear.

_____

_____

_____

_____

_____

54

11B | Olympic® dreams

NOUNS & ADJECTIVES (DESCRIBING PEOPLE)

1 Complete the dialogue with the best words.

Andrew: Did you use to play sport then, Geoff?

Geoff: Did I use to play sport!!! Andrew, I was king of the tennis court. I danced around the court like an angel.

Andrew: I guess you're not as (1) *agility / agile / agilely* as you used to be.

Geoff: It wasn't just about agility. It was about brain power, too. You needed the (2) *intelligence / intelligent / intelligently* to know what the other person was going to do next and the (3) *ruthlessness / ruthless / ruthlessly* to beat him into the ground.

Andrew: Goodness, Geoff! I've never heard you speak so (4) *enthusiasm / enthusiastic / enthusiastically* about anything! You should put that walking stick down before you break something.

Geoff: Yes, you didn't know me way back then. I used to train seven days a week because I was (5) *determination / determined / determinedly* to play at Wimbledon. Ah, yes, those were the days!

Andrew: I can't imagine you being so determined to be successful.

Geoff: Yes, no doubt about it. I had real (6) *ambition / ambitious / ambitiously*. You know I was at Centre Court.

Andrew: My goodness! You played at Centre Court in Wimbledon! Geoff, I never knew you were so (7) *talent / talented / talentless*!

Geoff: Oh, no … I didn't play there. I watched the great Fred Perry play there.

Andrew: Oh, I see. So, how about a game?

Geoff: Well, I'm not sure I have that kind of (8) *power / powerful / powerfully* any more.

VERBS WITH TWO OBJECTS

2 Rearrange the sentences so they mean the same as the first sentence.

1 The judges awarded two gold medals to the young Russian.
the young Russian   the judges
two gold medals   awarded .
The judges awarded the young Russian two gold medals.

2 The Queen gave the trophy to the winning team.
the winning team   gave   the trophy   the Queen .

_____

3 The Greeks built a massive Olympic® village for the athletes.
built   a massive   Olympic® village
the Greeks   the athletes .

_____

4 The athlete won a gold medal for her country.
medal   her country   the athlete   a gold   won .

_____

5 The winner gave a press conference to the journalists.
gave   the   a press   the winner   conference
journalists .

_____

TRANSLATION

3 Translate the sentences into your language.

1 Her combination of intelligence, power and natural talent have made her a world-class athlete.

_____.

2 Over 11,000 athletes gave their best to the world during the seventeen-day competition in Athens.

_____.

3 Thousands of rooms were built for the sportsmen and women by the Greek government.

_____.

4 Both of the Williams sisters were taught the basics of tennis from the age of four by their dad.

_____.

11c | Strange sports

CAUSATIVE

1 Rewrite the sentences using the words given and the causative.

1 A major company make his shirt, shorts and boots for him.
   He has _____.

2 On court, she wears dresses that a top fashion house designs for her.
   She has _____.

3 A major drinks company sponsors his bat and his cap.
   He has _____.

4 His sponsors deliver ten new racquets to his house every week.
   He has _____.

5 An apprentice player cleans his boots for him every time he plays in a match.
   He has _____.

6 An expert checks their bats after each inning to make sure they are in perfect condition.
   They have _____.

2 Match sentences 1–6 in exercise 1 to the sports a–c.

a tennis   __
b baseball __
c football __

SERVICES

3 Complete the article with verbs from the box in the correct form.

| design   cook   cut   deliver |
| test   iron   service   serve |

After winning £24 million, Mary Hinge decided to stop playing championship tennis. 'I've become the laziest person in the world,' she says proudly. 'I worked hard for years and now I don't do anything! I have my breakfast (1) _____ to me in bed every morning. In fact, I have all of my food (2) _____ for me. If I want something special, I let Jane, my housekeeper, know and she phones the supermarket and has the food (3) _____ to the door. Oh, and I love clothes, you know. I have everything (4) _____ for me in Italy. I wear each item of clothing once, then I have it washed and (5) _____ before I give it away to charity.

The ex-champion goes on to tell me about her plans for today. 'My hair's a bit long, so I'm having it (6) _____ at twelve. Oh, and I need to have the car (7) _____. But Jane can do that. Oh, and my eye test! Jane can't do that. I'll have to have my eyes (8) _____ without her!'

🔵 DICTATION

4 🔵 **42** Write the text that you hear.

_____

_____

_____

_____

11D | Sport relief

MAKE & DO

1 Complete the dialogue with the correct forms of *make* and *do*.

Simon: I'm going (1) _____ a cup of coffee. Do you want to have a break?

Nicola: No thanks, darling. I have (2) _____ these accounts and email them by 3pm. But I've (3) _____ a mistake somewhere. It's driving me crazy!

Simon: Oh, poor you. I'm going (4) _____ some shopping and I'll (5) _____ a delicious dinner for the two of us tonight. OK?

Nicola: Oh, that would be lovely, but I can't really stop for dinner. I have some other work (6) _____ after this.

Simon: You should (7) _____ some sport and make some time for your family.

Nicola: OK, OK, you're right. If you're going out, could you (8) _____ me a favour and take this plant round to my mother?

QUESTION TAGS (CHECKING)

2 Complete the dialogue with question tags from the box.

| won't you | are you | aren't you | can't you |
| could we | won't you | haven't you | |

David: You're going to run in the marathon, (1) _____?

John: Yes. I have to get more sponsors though.

David: You can ask your company, (2) _____?

John: Already have. They promised to double anything I raise.

David: That's generous. You've asked your friends, (3) _____?

John: Most of them. Hey, we couldn't ask your parents, (4) _____?

David: Why not? You'll ask your parents, too, (5) _____?

John: They haven't got much money.

David: Oh, come on! You're not asking for a fortune, (6) _____?

John: No, that's true. By the way, you'll sponsor me, (7) _____?

David: I might … if you're nice to me.

3 Complete the dialogue with question tags.

Adrian: So what's 'Sport Relief'? It's a charity, (1) _____?

Brian: Yes. It raises money to run projects that use sports to help kids. You've heard about it though, (2) _____?

Adrian: Yeah, but not much. What'll happen to the money? It goes to people in the UK, (3) _____?

Brian: No, only 50% does. The other half goes overseas to projects in places like Africa or Asia.

Adrian: That's good. I imagine you've got lots of famous people involved. I guess you couldn't do this without celebrities, (4) _____?

Brian: No, no, that's not true. Of course we've got big names, but we couldn't do it without ordinary people. In 2010, the charity raised over £30 million.

Adrian: Wow! So you're going to run the marathon this year, (5) _____?

Brian: It only happens every two years. Hey, you could run it next year, (6) _____?

Adrian: Me? No way!! I will watch it on TV though.

TRANSLATION

4 Translate the advert into your language.

Helping Hand is here to help you raise money for charities. There are hundreds of ways of doing that. The most popular way is by being sponsored to do something. Once you have the idea, you find people to sponsor you. So whether you run a marathon or swim a mile, you can make a difference to someone's life. *Helping Hand* is here to help you find a way.

_____

_____

_____

_____

11 | Reading

BRITAIN'S MOST UNUSUAL SPORTING EVENT

The Brits have always been obsessed by sport. The modern sports of football and rugby were first played in the public schools of England; tennis was invented in London and golf had been played on the wild
5 coast of Scotland long before the rest of the world took to the sport. Britain is, however, also home to some seriously bizarre and rather less well-known sporting events. And one of the most bizarre of all is the *Man versus Horse* marathon …
10 Every June, in the small Welsh town of Llanwrtyd Wells, men, women, cyclists and horses race against each other over an extremely demanding twenty-two mile course which crosses some of the most beautiful countryside in Wales. The first race was
15 organized in 1980 by the landlord of a pub called the Neuadd Arms. Depending on who you ask, there are two stories of how he got the idea. One story says that he was inspired by the 18th century tale of the
20 famous Welsh runner Guto Nyth Bran, who was reported to have raced against a horse in the county of Cardiganshire and won. Another story says that the landlord overheard a conversation between two
25 customers, one of whom was arguing that a man could beat a horse in a race, and it seemed like a good idea to find out whether he was right.

In the early years of the event, horses always won. However, in 1989, a horse was beaten for the first time by
30 a human when the cyclist Tim Gould came in first. At that time, nobody really believed that a human runner would one day win the race, but the challenge of trying to beat a horse was so great that the sporting event grew bigger and bigger each year. A race that had started as a bit of fun
35 started to attract serious athletes from all over the world. Another important factor in the growth in popularity of the event was the prize money on offer. In 1980, the event organizers had offered £1,000 to a human who won the race. In 2004, when the race was held for the twenty-fifth
40 time, £25,000 was offered to the winning human.

It was, perhaps, inevitable that somebody would have the ambition, determination and talent to defy logic and beat the four-legged athletes to the finish. That man was Huw Lobb who, on a hot day in June 2004, crossed the line two
45 minutes ahead of the fastest horse. Huw was no fun runner – he was an experienced marathon runner who had run well in the London Marathon earlier that year. Even so, it was an amazing achievement, and one that shows that whenever someone sets a challenge there is
50 always somebody tough enough to rise to it.

1 Read the article and decide if the sentences are true (T) or false (F). Correct the false sentences.

1 According to the writer, Britain has a significant sporting legacy. ___
2 The race takes place on the streets of the town of Llanwrtyd Wells. ___
3 It isn't clear exactly what inspired the pub landlord to start the event. ___
4 The first human runner to beat a horse was Tim Gould in 1989. ___
5 Every year, the event has grown in size and prestige. ___
6 Humans have still not managed to beat a horse in the race. ___

2 Read the article again and write short answers to the questions.

1 Where was golf invented?
2 When does the *Man versus Horse* race take place each year?
3 When did the race first take place?
4 Which legendary runner may have inspired the pub landlord?
5 What two factors resulted in the growth in popularity of the event?
6 Apart from winning this race, what had Huw Lobb also achieved in 2004?

3 Find words or phrases in the text that mean the same as the definitions 1–9. The paragraph numbers are in brackets.

1 very strongly interested in (1)
2 very strange (1)
3 very difficult (2)
4 listened to a conversation that you were not part of (2)
5 to make people want to be a part of something (3)
6 always going to happen (4)
7 difficult (4)

🔊 READ & LISTEN

4 🔊 **43** Listen to Reading 11 *Britain's most unusual sporting event* on the CD and read the article again.

12A | Basic needs

REPORTED SPEECH & THOUGHT

1 Rearrange the reported sentences to find out what happened to Richard.

1 him the previous day   had phoned   his father's   solicitor   Richard said that   she had   some good   news   to say .

Richard said that his father's solicitor had phoned him the previous day to say she had some good news.

2 two sports cars   his father   Richard that   had left   him four   she told   million pounds and .

_____

3 know what to   drink to   say   Richard   that he didn't   going to   but he was   his father that night   said .

_____

4 he hadn't spoken   for ten years   he told   his father   the solicitor   to .

_____

5 could finally   debts   he said   off his   that he   pay .

_____

6 rest of   he told   a homeless charity   the solicitor   he would   the money to   give the .

_____

7 him a house   said that   his father   had also   with fourteen bedrooms   the solicitor   given .

_____

2 Rewrite the sentences in exercise 1 in direct speech.

1 *'My father's solicitor phoned me yesterday to say she had some good news.'*

2 '_____ ,'

3 '_____ ,'

4 '_____ ,'

5 '_____ ,'

6 '_____ ,'

7 '_____ ,'

3 Find and correct one mistake in each sentence.

1 She told to me that her family and friends were the most important thing for her.

2 He said he wanted that a steady job more than anything.

3 He told that the most important thing was to have someone in his life.

4 She says me that you couldn't live without money.

5 She said that her daughter had been ill at the moment and the most important thing was that she'd be OK in the future.

6 He said that he is wanting a roof over his head more than anything.

VOCABULARY FROM THE LESSON

4 Underline the word or phrase that does not go with the verb.

1 **give someone**   money   something to eat   to fly home   hope

2 **lose**   your job   your time   your home   your family and friends

3 **be**   responsible for someone or something   a heroin addict   homeless   fall in love

4 **have**   a steady job   homeless   a roof over your head   money in your pocket

5 **take**   money from someone   a mortgage   drugs   a plane home

6 **chat**   over coffee   with neighbours   between hours   to your friends

🅐 DICTATION

5 🅐 **44** Write the text that you hear.

_____

_____

_____

_____

_____

_____

_____

12B | Money

REPORTED QUESTIONS

1 Complete the dialogue with the correct verb forms.

Maria: Hey, I bumped into Jane Watts yesterday. Remember her?

Ray: Sure. I've been told that she's a rich woman now.

Maria: Yes, very! She asked me if I still (1) *had seen / saw* you.

Ray: Really!? And what did you tell her?

Maria: I said that we (2) *were still seeing / had seen* each other on a regular basis.

Ray: Uh-huh.

Maria: And then she asked me where (3) *did you live / you lived*.

Ray: No way!

Maria: Yeah. And listen to this. She wanted to know whether I thought you (4) *will / would* like to see her.

Ray: OK. Stop it. This isn't funny!

Maria: Wait … wait. I told her that you (5) *were / had been* married now.

Ray: And she wanted to know who I was married to, right?

Maria: Right! And when I said you (6) *had been married / were married* to me for 20 years, guess what she said?

Ray: Did she say she thought I (7) *will be doing / would do* better?

Maria: Do you want this soup in the dish, or on your head? She said I was a lucky woman.

Ray: I wish I was as lucky as you … in the dish, honey, in the dish!

VOCABULARY FROM THE LESSON

2 Match the verbs 1–8 to the words they go with a–h.

1	win	a	in debt
2	earn	b	money on myself
3	spend	c	a salary
4	be	d	a prize
5	donate	e	money for a rainy day
6	lend	f	money to charity
7	save	g	money in stocks and shares
8	invest	h	money to friends

TRANSLATION

3 Translate the text into your language.

I got an interesting advertisement through my door the other day. It asked me if I would like to become a millionaire. Of course I would, I thought. Then the advertisement said the best way to get rich was to marry someone rich, inherit money or win the lottery. It then asked if any of these things had happened to me. I said, 'No'. It seemed to know the answer anyway, because then it told me not to worry. All I had to do was ring the number at the end of the advertisement.

_____

_____

_____

_____

_____

_____.

12c | Sue!

TELL & ASK WITH INFINITIVE

1 Choose the correct words or phrases to complete the text.

On his first date with Eva Fischer, 52-year-old Rudy Cox declared his love and asked (1) *her / to her / she* to marry him. Eva told him (2) *don't / not / not to* be ridiculous, but she agreed to see him again. On their next date, Rudy repeated his request and gave her a ten-dollar engagement ring, but asked her (3) *not / not to / to not* give her answer immediately. Eva asked him (4) *stop / stopping / to stop* talking about marriage, but on their next date, Rudy again (5) *asked / said / told* Eva to be his wife. Eva had had enough. She told him not (6) *call / to call / to calling* her any more and that the relationship was over.

The next day, Eva received a letter from Rudy asking (7) *her / her to / to her* return the ring. She didn't reply and, in any case, she had thrown the ring away. Two weeks later, another letter arrived. In it, Rudy told (8) *Eva / to Eva / to her* to return the ring within two days or he would sue her for emotional distress and the loss of the ring. Alternatively, he added, she could agree to be his wife.

2 Complete the second sentence so that it means the same as the first.

1 'Can you explain the nature of your injuries?' the judge asked the plaintiff.

The judge _____ the nature of his injuries.

2 The judge said, 'The company must pay $20,000 in damages.'

The judge _____ $20,000 in damages.

3 'Please don't forget the emotional distress of my client,' the lawyer asked the court.

The lawyer _____ forget the emotional distress of his client.

4 'Sue them for as much as possible!' she said to her lawyer.

She _____ them for as much as possible.

5 'Don't accept an out-of-court settlement,' said the lawyer to her client.

The lawyer told _____ accept an out-of-court settlement.

6 'Could you speak a little more loudly?' the judge asked the plaintiff.

The judge _____ a little more loudly

REPORTING VERBS

3 Match the words 1–5 to the definitions a–f.

1	to claim	a	to tell someone about a possible problem so they can avoid it or deal with it
2	to insist	b	to say that you are not satisfied with something
3	to complain	c	to officially tell someone something
4	to inform	d	to say that something is true, even if there is no definite proof
5	to deny	e	to say that you did not do something that someone has accused you of doing
6	to warn	f	to say very strongly that something is true

Extracts adapted from *Macmillan English Dictionary For Advanced Learners.*

4 Complete the sentences with a verb from the box in the correct form.

deny	complain	warn	inform	insist

1 The teenager _____ responsibility for stealing the tank – he said his friends had taken it.

2 The airline _____ the passengers that it was a non-smoking flight.

3 She _____ that her new computer wasn't working properly.

4 He _____ again and again that she wasn't the right woman for him, but she wouldn't believe him.

5 The children were _____ not to swim in the lake because of the currents.

12D | Golden moments

SOCIAL EXPRESSIONS

1 Choose the best reply a–c to the situations 1–5.

1 Your friend's ten-year-old has just passed her piano exam. You say:
a) Thank you very much.   b) Well done!
c) Take care.

2 The train is crowded and you need to get off. You say:
a) Sorry.   b) Excuse me.   c) Pardon?

3 You knocked your work colleague's papers on the floor. You say:
a) Thank you very much.   b) Excuse me.   c) Sorry.

4 You phone a friend to say you'll be at her place in ten minutes. You say:
a) Well done!   b) Take care.   c) See you soon.

5 You say goodbye to a friend you won't see for a while. You say:
a) See you soon.   b) Take care.   c) Have a nice day.

2 Match the expressions a–g to the situations 1–7.

1 A good friend is leaving to go back to his country.
2 Your neighbour tells you that she didn't get the job she applied for.
3 You invited a friend for dinner, but he/she is busy.
4 You and your neighbour both have job interviews tomorrow. Your neighbour wishes you luck.
5 Your next-door neighbour tells you that his wife fell over and broke her arm.
6 Your good friends tell you that the offer they put in for a new house has just been accepted.
7 You are chatting to a friend on the phone when you remember that you have an appointment.

☐ a Oh well, never mind. Another day, maybe?
☐ b The same to you.
☐ c Excellent news! Congratulations.
☐ d Well, I must be going. I've got a dentist's appointment.
☐ e Oh, what a shame. That's really bad luck.
☐ f Oh no, that's really bad luck. Is she OK?
☐ g We'll miss you. Keep in touch, OK?

VOCABULARY FROM THE LESSON

3 Match the verbs 1–8 to the words they go with a–h.

1	get	a	your time
2	take	b	after yourself
3	have	c	married
4	look	d	a chat
5	keep	e	round for dinner
6	come	f	care of yourself
7	have	g	a safe journey
8	take	h	my fingers crossed

🔊 DICTATION

4 🔊 **45** Write the text that you hear.

_____

_____

_____

_____

12 | Reading

LATE ONE SUNDAY AFTERNOON in September 1999, Oseola
McCarty, an elderly cleaning lady, passed away in the little wooden frame
house where she had lived and worked most of her life. It may seem like an
ordinary end to a humble life, but there was something quite exceptional about
5 this woman.

In the summer of 1995, McCarty gave $150,000, most of the money she had
saved throughout her life, to the University of Southern Mississippi in her
hometown. The money was to help other African Americans through university.
10 She had started her savings habit as a young child when she would return
from school to clean and iron for money which she would then save.

She led a simple, frugal existence, never spending on anything but her most
basic needs. Her bank also advised her on investing her hard-earned savings.

When she retired, she decided that she wanted to use the money to give
15 children of limited means the opportunity to go to university. She had wanted
to become a nurse, but had to leave school to look after ill relatives and work.
When asked why she had given her life savings away, she replied, 'I'm giving
it away so that children won't have to work so hard, like I did.'

After news of her donation hit the media, over 600 donations were made to
20 the scholarship fund. One was given by media executive, Ted Turner, who
reputedly gave a billion dollars.

She didn't want any fuss made over her gift, but the news got out and she was
invited all over the United States to talk to people. Wherever she went, people
would come up to her to say a few words or to just touch her. She met the
25 ordinary and the famous, President Clinton included. In the last few years of
her life, before she died of cancer, McCarty was given over 300 awards: she
was honoured by the United Nations and received the Presidential Citizen's
Medal. Despite having no real education, she found herself with two honorary
doctorates: one from the University of Southern Mississippi and the other from
30 Harvard University. Her generosity was clearly an inspiration to many and
proof that true selflessness does exist.

---

1 Read the article. Complete the sentences with the best
ending, a, b or c.

1 This woman shocked and inspired the world because …
   a) she had managed to save so much money.
   b) she gave her money to African Americans. c) she
   gave her life savings to help others through university.
2 She managed to save so much money because …
   a) she had ironed and washed clothes all her life.
   b) she had worked hard, saved hard and invested
   carefully. c) she had opened a good bank account.
3 She gave her money away because …
   a) she wanted to help the university. b) she wanted
   others to have the chance to become nurses.
   c) she wanted others to have the opportunity to escape
   a hard life.
4 When her generosity was made public …
   a) people donated billions.
   b) hundreds of students got scholarships.
   c) hundreds of people put money into the fund.
5 McCarty became famous because …
   a) she had saved $150,000. b) of her generosity.
   c) she travelled all over America.
6 People responded to her by …
   a) honouring her in different ways. b) introducing her
   to President Clinton. c) sending her to university.

2 Match the words and phrases from the article 1–5 to
the best definition a–c. The line numbers are in
brackets.

1 passed away (2) a) lived b) spent a lot of time c) died
2 a humble life (4) a) a life which is poor
   b) a life which doesn't try to be better than others
   c) a life which was not exceptional
3 frugal (12) a) only spending money on essentials
   b) only spending money on cheap things
   c) only saving money
4 honorary doctorates (28–29) a) specialist doctors to
   help her
   b) degrees in recognition of someone's life and/or work
   c) free places to study at the universities
5 selflessness (31) a) only thinking about yourself
   b) not thinking about other people
   c) not thinking about yourself

READ & LISTEN

3 🔘 **46** Listen to Reading 12 on the CD and read the
article again.

1 | A description of a best friend

Me and my best friend

1 My best mate is Greg. (1) *I first met him* at school over 20 years ago when we were eleven. I remember that it was in the playground while we were playing football. (2) *To begin with, he seemed* very arrogant, and I didn't like him at all. But he made a joke about what a terrible footballer I was, and it was so funny that I had to laugh. We've been close friends ever since, although there have been times when we haven't seen each other for years.

2 Many people find it hard to understand Greg. (3) *He comes across as being* very serious, but he loves having fun and meeting people. He's really good company and he's got a great sense of humour, although he doesn't like telling jokes. He's also a very good listener. Over the years he has helped me when I've had a problem by sitting and listening. Because he's very easy to talk to, we chat for hours about stuff like football, politics and relationships.

3 Physically, he is average build and quite tall. He has got a pale complexion and blond curly hair, but (4) *the first thing you notice about him is* his moustache. (5) *I wouldn't describe him* as good-looking, but he has an interesting face. He has lively blue eyes and a prominent nose that lots of women seem to like.

4 (6) *He's into* lots of things, especially music, but he hates dancing! (7) *He's got a real talent for* the guitar and he plays a lot when he's alone at home. He is quite an active guy and he enjoys sport, although he can't play football any more. He loves going out to concerts, the pub and exhibitions. One of his greatest loves is food and wine. Now that's another reason why I like him so much – he's an excellent cook!

READING

1 Read the article and match the paragraphs 1–4 to the headings a–d.

- ☐ a What he looks like
- ☐ b What he likes
- ☐ c What he is like
- ☐ d How we met

2 Look at the writer's plan for the article. Cross out the three pieces of information which he did not include in the article.

1	2
don't see each other all the time / met at school / arrogant / much bigger than me / joke about me	seems serious / really fun / good company / hates telling jokes / good listener / we chat a lot / a bit impatient
3	4
the moustache! / looks like his father / blue eyes / women like his nose / height / pale / hair	guitar / dancing Ugh! / sport / his cooking / concerts, etc

LANGUAGE FOCUS

1 Match the phrases in italics in the article 1–7 to the phrases a–g.

- ☐ a At first, I thought he was
- ☐ b He gives the impression of being
- ☐ c He's really good at
- ☐ d He's really keen on
- ☐ e His most prominent feature is
- ☐ f The first time we met was at
- ☐ g You can't really say that he's

2 Complete the phrases in exercise 1 about your best friend. Change *he* to *she* if necessary.

3 Insert capital letters and full stops in the paragraph below.

> physically, he is average build and quite tall he has got a pale complexion and blond curly hair, but the first thing you notice about him is his moustache I wouldn't describe him as good-looking, but he has an interesting face he has lively blue eyes and a prominent nose that lots of women seem to like

Check your answers in the article.

4 Use the notes below to write a short paragraph. Choose the best order in which to present the information.

> Dave / short / in his forties / fair hair / going a little bald / very fit / old-fashioned clothes / still thinks he's good-looking! / small round glasses / muscular

5 Check that you have included capital letters and full stops in the correct places in the paragraph that you wrote for exercise 4.

WRITING

1 Use the paragraph organization in Reading exercise 2 to write a plan for a text about your best friend.

1	2
3	4

2 Look at your plan and decide ...

• if there is any extra information that you want to include.
• if there is any information that you do not want to include.
• the best order to present the information in each of the paragraphs.

3 Write an article entitled 'My best friend'. Use the points below to help you.

1 Look again at the phrases in Language focus exercise 1 and in the article about Greg. Do you want to use any of these phrases in your article?
2 Check that you have used capital letters and full stops where necessary.

Madrid

(1) ____ Visitors are attracted by the city's history, excellent museums, wonderful food and unbelievable nightlife. Add marvellous weather and the open friendliness of its people and it's not too difficult to understand why Madrid is one of the most popular places to visit in Europe.

(2) ____ Madrid was just a small town in the centre of Spain until King Philip II made it the capital in 1561. The city rapidly became the political and cultural centre of Spain. One of the most popular places with visitors is the impressive Plaza Mayor (Main Square), which was built in Madrid's early days. Other interesting historical landmarks include the Royal Palace and the Cibeles Fountain (18th century), and the Toledo Arch, a national monument built in 1817. When the weather is good, why not escape the city and spend some time in the beautiful Retiro Park? Families with young children will enjoy strolling around the park or boating on the lake.

(3) ____ A must for all visitors is the spectacular Prado Museum with its first-rate collection of European art. If you have a little more time, you should definitely go to the Thyssen-Bornemisza Museum and the Queen Sofia National Centre for the Arts. Apart from these three exceptional museums, there are a lot of smaller art museums housing superb collections.

(4) ____ Many Madrileños (i.e. people from Madrid) love going out to the cinema, the theatre or a concert. Others enjoy going from one bar to another, meeting friends along the way. Food is really important to people here and you can eat very well in bars, cafés and restaurants. The city has an outstanding live music scene and the choice is enormous: rock, pop, flamenco, reggae, hip hop, and much more. For people looking for a night out, there are hundreds of clubs and many of them are open all night. People here enjoy life and there is definitely something for everyone.

READING

1 Read the text about Madrid and choose where you would see it 1–3.

1 a history book
2 a guidebook
3 a description of a holiday

2 Complete the spaces 1–4 with the topic sentences a–d.

a If you love history, Madrid has a lot to offer.
b Madrid is famous for its nightlife and at night the city explodes into action.
c Madrid is the capital of Spain and a great destination for a short weekend break or for a longer trip.
d The city is well known for its marvellous art museums.

3 Tick the information that is included in the text.

1 There are many good reasons for visitors to go to Madrid.
2 It's easy to get around the city on the public transport system.
3 Madrid was not always an important city.
4 Tourists like going to the city's Main Square.
5 The city has a rich collection of museums.
6 Madrid has first-class shopping centres, as well as many interesting small shops.
7 There are plenty of things to do in the evening.
8 Sports fans should try to get tickets for a football match at the Bernabéu Stadium.
9 People who enjoy good food will not be disappointed.

LANGUAGE FOCUS

1 Complete the phrases so that they are true for a town or city in your country.

1 One of the most popular places with visitors is …
2 Other interesting historical landmarks include …
3 When the weather is good, why not …
4 Families with young children will enjoy …
5 A must for all visitors is the …
6 If you have a little more time, you should definitely …
7 For people looking for a night out, there are …

2 Look at the thesaurus box and find the adjectives in the text about Madrid. Which nouns do the adjectives describe?

Thesaurus: English (UK)	
Looked up	Replace with synonym
excellent (adj.)	wonderful unbelievable outstanding exceptional superb marvellous impressive spectacular first-rate

3 For each adjective in the thesaurus box, write the name of something you could describe in a town or city in your country.

4 Read the information in the box.

> **Use capital letters for …**
> * names of people and places.
>   *Madrid, Toledo Arch*
> * countries, nationality adjectives and languages.
>   *Spain, Spanish*
> * titles.
>   *King Philip II, Queen Sofia, Dr Gardner,*
>   *Sir Elton John*
> * days of the week and months of the year.
>   *Saturday, December*

5 Rewrite the text using capital letters where necessary.

> If you're in brussels in april or may, don't miss a visit to the royal palace at laeken with its beautiful gardens and greenhouses. The greenhouses were built for king leopold II of belgium, who was also responsible for the nearby japanese tower, which sometimes houses temporary exhibitions.

WRITING

1 You are going to write a guide to your town or city, using the following instructions.

1 Choose a town or city in your country and make notes about its attractions to visitors.
2 Organize your notes into three paragraphs.
3 Select the three or four most important reasons for visitors to come to this place and write a short introductory paragraph.
4 Then write the three paragraphs that you planned in point 2.

Below are some notes on paragraph writing.

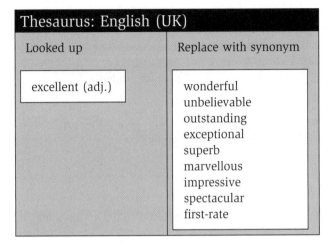

> When we begin a new paragraph, we can (1) leave a line before starting the new paragraph, or (2) leave a short space at the beginning of the new paragraph.
>
> > responsible for the nearby Japanese Tower, which sometimes houses temporary exhibitions.
> >
> > Another interesting place to visit outside the town
>
> > responsible for the nearby Japanese Tower, which sometimes houses temporary exhibitions.
> > Another interesting place to visit outside the town

2 Look at what you have written. Can you improve it in any way?

1 Are there any phrases in Language focus exercise 1 that you could use in your guide?
2 Have you used an interesting variety of adjectives?
3 Check that you have used capital letters and full stops where necessary.

3 | Advantages and disadvantages

There are a lot of advantages to living on a university campus. For a start, life is usually cheaper. For example, food and accommodation are often subsidized by the university and students who live off campus have to pay normal prices for everything. Secondly, you don't have to deal with things that go wrong in rented accommodation, such as washing machines breaking down or gas cookers that don't work properly. The most important reason for living on campus is the time you save being so close to places like the library. As a result, you have much more time to study.

However, there are some disadvantages, too. First of all, it is easy to spend all your time on campus and because of that you can lose contact with the 'real world'. What is more, you don't have as much independence or freedom on campus as off. For instance, you normally can't choose what and when to eat. Finally, if you live on campus, it isn't necessary to develop the same life skills as you do living off campus – skills like managing the day-to-day running of a house.

To sum up, I believe that the main reason for being at university is to study. Living on campus allows students more time to study without the distractions and responsibilities of rented accommodation. As a result, I would recommend people to live on campus if they have the chance.

READING

1 Read the composition and choose the best summary 1–4.

1 It is better for students to live off campus.
2 There is no important difference between living on and off campus.
3 Living on campus is better for students.
4 On or off campus?

2 What reasons does the writer give (1) for and (2) against living on campus?

LANGUAGE FOCUS

1 Find five words or expressions in the composition to complete the table.

ordering points in a composition		
making your first point	making additional points	making your final point
Firstly, In the first place, _____ _____	Moreover, On top of that, _____ _____	Lastly, _____

2 In the paragraph below, insert expressions from exercise 1 so that the text is easier to follow.

There are many good reasons for studying a foreign language in the country of the language. You are surrounded by the language and can learn a lot without really making any effort. There are many opportunities to learn about the culture, and this can be extremely interesting. The progress that you make will probably be much faster.

3 Correct nine spelling mistakes in the sentences below.

1 It normaly costs a lot of money to study in a foreign country.
2 I beleive that it is often a good idea to find accomodation with a host family.
3 It is usualy neccesary to plan your stay very carefully.
4 With more independance, you may also have responsabilities which you do not have at home.
5 I would certainly reccomend looking for a part-time job during your stay.
6 With so much to do, manageing your time can be difficult.

Find the correct spellings in the composition about living on campus.

WRITING

1 Look at the title of a composition and the notes that a writer has made. Mark the notes A (advantages) or D (disadvantages).

The advantages and disadvantages of studying abroad

1 Make new friends/meet different kinds of people ___
2 No support from family and friends when things go wrong ___
3 Learn about a new culture ___
4 Foreign language may cause problems ___
5 Difficult to study with so many distractions ___
6 Improve your foreign language skills ___
7 Looks good on your CV ___
8 Helps to develop self-confidence ___
9 Usually more expensive ___
10 Hard to adapt to different food and customs ___

---

2 Choose three advantages and three disadvantages that you think are the most important. What is the best order in which to present these ideas?

3 Write a composition called *The advantages and disadvantages of studying abroad*.

Paragraph 1: present the advantages
Paragraph 2: present the disadvantages
Paragraph 3: sum up the argument and give your personal opinion

Use the points below to help you.

1 Remember to use a variety of expressions to present the order of your arguments.
2 Check your spelling. If you are using a computer, set the computer language to English and use the spelling checker.
3 Check that you have used capital letters and full stops where necessary.

STUDY ABROAD

Beijing, China	London, England	Bonn, Germany
Dublin, Ireland	Oxford, England	Rome, Italy
Kenya, East Africa	Paris, France	Washington, DC

4 | A narrative: lottery winner

The UK's BIGGEST Lottery Win

1   'Ooh, I've won. That's nice,' Iris Jeffrey said to her family when she learned that she had become the UK's biggest-ever lottery winner, with a jackpot of £20.1 million. However, the Belfast woman almost missed out on her big win. She had put the winning ticket in a cupboard and forgotten about it. It was only a month later when she was watching TV with her husband, Robert, that she heard that the winner of a jackpot had not claimed their prize. She checked her numbers and found that she had all six correct. At first, the mother-of-two still couldn't believe she had won, and she asked her daughter, Wendy, to check again. In the end, she had to accept the news. 'I had a glass of milk and went to bed,' said the lucky winner when she described her reaction to becoming a multi-millionaire.

2   For 58-year-old Iris, the win came at an important time. Earlier this year, she discovered that she was suffering from cancer. She was waiting for an operation when her numbers came up, so the money will help in her fight against the disease. Elder daughter Wendy told reporters, 'With all the money, we can go anywhere in the world to get the very best treatment.'

3   With her winnings, the UK's latest winner says that she wants to look after her friends and family. Her younger daughter, Karen, is expecting a baby, and the grandmother-to-be is looking forward to spoiling them both. First of all, however, she plans to buy a new washing machine. After that, there will be a new car for Robert. And finally, she would like to go to Las Vegas with her husband. Having just heard from her doctor that the cancer is responding well to treatment, Mrs Jeffrey now has two reasons to celebrate.

READING

1   Read the newspaper article about a lottery winner and match the paragraphs 1–3 to the summaries a–c.

☐ a   What she plans to do with the money
☐ b   How she won
☐ c   The winner and why the win was so special

2   Put the events in the correct order.

☐ Her health improved.
☐ She decided how to spend the money.
☐ She discovered that she had won the jackpot.
☐ She had a glass of milk to celebrate.
☐ Iris Jeffrey learned that she had cancer.
☐ She put her lottery ticket in a cupboard.
☐ She watched TV with her husband.

3   Match the things people said 1–5 to the people a–e.

1   'Good news! Things seem to be improving.'
2   'Yes, I'd love a new BMW.'
3   'I've got something to tell you both – I'm pregnant.'
4   'It could be me – wait a minute – I'll go and find that ticket.'
5   'Yes, you've definitely got all six numbers, mum.'

☐ a   Robert to Iris
☐ b   Iris to Robert
☐ c   Wendy to Iris
☐ d   doctor to Iris
☐ e   Karen to Iris and Robert

LANGUAGE FOCUS

1   Read the information in the box.

> We use *first of all*, *at first* and *initially* to talk about the first of a series of actions. *At first* and *initially* suggest a contrast with later actions.
>
> *First of all, she plans to buy a new washing machine.*
>
> *At first, she couldn't believe she had won.*
>
> We use *finally*, *in the end* and *eventually* to talk about the last of a series of actions. *In the end* and *eventually* suggest that the series of actions was long or difficult.
>
> *Finally, she would like to go to Las Vegas.*
>
> *In the end, she had to accept the news.*

2 Choose the best expressions to complete the text.

> A few years ago, I started buying lottery tickets. (1) *At first / First of all*, my husband thought it was a waste of money, but then I started winning. (2) *Eventually / First of all*, I won just a small amount – £50 – but then I got another £40 two weeks later. My husband still thought it was stupid. I continued to win small amounts, but after four months, I (3) *finally / initially* won quite a lot – £2,000. After winning nine times in six months, my husband (4) *at first / eventually* agreed that the lottery wasn't such a bad thing after all.

3 In order to avoid repeating 'Iris Jeffrey', the writer uses seven other ways to refer to her, other than 'she'. Find and underline them.

4 Use your imagination to replace the words in italics.

> Richard Pratt appeared in court yesterday with debts of over £90,000. *Richard Pratt* had spent it all on the lottery. He first tried his luck with a single ticket over a year ago, but each week he gambled more and more.
> After spending more than £500 a week on tickets, *Richard Pratt* soon ran out of money. Sure that he would soon have a lucky break, *Richard Pratt* sold his car and, finally, his house. Outside the court, *Richard Pratt* told reporters, 'It wasn't worth it.'

5 Look at the examples. Then rewrite sentences 1–6 with correct punctuation and capital letters.

'I had a glass of milk and went to bed,' said the lucky winner.
Wendy told reporters, 'With all the money, we can go anywhere in the world.'

1 And the final winning number is 49 said the man on the radio
2 I thought I'd give it a go, but I never thought I'd win he said
3 I used my parents' birthdays to choose the numbers he explained
4 He turned round to his passenger and said I've just won the lottery
5 You're kidding he said
6 The most incredible thing happened to me today he told his wife

WRITING

1 You are going to write the story of another lottery winner. Divide the information below into two paragraphs.

> John Townsend / 24 / taxi driver / from Glasgow, Scotland / prize £15 million / never played before / the six numbers were his mother and father's birthdays / driving in taxi / heard lottery results on the radio / had to stop his taxi because he was so shocked / explained to passenger / asked him to take another cab

2 Write the story.

Use the information in exercise 1 for the first two paragraphs.

Decide the order in which you want to present this information.

Use your imagination in the third paragraph to decide what he did (or plans to do) with the money.

Use the points below to help you.

1 Remember to use a variety of ways to refer to Mr Townsend.
2 Check all the past tenses (past simple, past continuous, past perfect) that you have used.
3 Remember to use time expressions to show the connections between different events.
4 Check your spelling and punctuation.

5 | An advertisement

TO RUSSIA WITH LOVE

Travelling to Moscow or St Petersburg?

Looking for low fares & quality services?

1. MillanAir's reliable and efficient new service between London Heathrow and Russia offers you unbeatable choice at unbeatable value. Two departures a day, seven days a week, 52 weeks a year. With a journey time of just under four hours, you'll be in Russia before you know it.

   For travellers going further, our network of partner airlines provides a full range of onward flight connections.

2. And like any good airline, we also offer hotel booking, travel insurance and car hire services. All of this at discount rates.

   For convenience, comfort and care, fly MillanAir.

3. With MillanAir's modern fleet of stylish A320 aircraft, you are sure to arrive relaxed and happy, and our in-flight service is second to none. And naturally, we are more than happy to look after passengers with special needs.

4. You can rely on us to make your journey a memorable experience. Delicious meals prepared by top-class chefs. An incredible choice of ten music channels and the very latest movies. Duty-free shopping at unbelievable prices. And if there's anything we've forgotten, our friendly and professional staff will be only too pleased to help.

5. Whether you're travelling on business or for pleasure, MillanAir is the choice for you. With prices starting at £150 one way, you won't find a better deal. But that's only the beginning. Regular flyer discounts. Early booking reductions of 10%. Last-minute offers.

   It all adds up to one thing: we'll take you to Russia with love.

   MILLANAIR.COM

READING

1. Read the advertisement and match the paragraphs 1–5 to the headings a–e.

   ☐ a Food and entertainment
   ☐ b Other services
   ☐ c Prices
   ☐ d Routes and connections
   ☐ e Type of aircraft

2. Compare the MillanAir service with the service of Wilson Air, another company. Mark each feature *M* (if MillanAir's service is better) or *W* (if Wilson Air's service is better).

> ### Wilson Air
>
> Direct flights to four top destinations (Moscow, St Petersburg, Novosibirsk, Vladivostok) ____
> Ten flights a day ____
> Journey time 4 hours 10 minutes ____
> Basic fare £180 ____
> Free travel insurance ____
> Book early and get 5% off ____
> Sandwiches and snacks served on board ____

LANGUAGE FOCUS

1. Complete the adjectives by putting the missing letters in the spaces.

   1 r e l i _ _ _ _
   2 e f f i c i _ _ _
   3 u n b e a t _ _ _ _
   4 s t y l _ _ _
   5 m e m o r _ _ _ _
   6 d e l i c _ _ _ _
   7 i n c r e d _ _ _ _
   8 u n b e l i e v _ _ _ _

   Check your answers in the advertisement for MillanAir.

2 English sentences contain a subject and a main verb. Which of the following are not full sentences?

1 Journey time only 30 hours.
2 Light meals are served on board.
3 Our award-winning website makes booking easy.
4 Prices start at an unbelievable £60 one way.
5 Special rates for group travel.
6 Total satisfaction guaranteed or your money back.
7 We never forget you have a choice.

3 Rewrite the phrases below as full sentences with a subject and a verb. Use the words in the boxes to help you.

Subjects

there	we	you

Verbs

is	are	offer

1 Two departures a day, seven days a week, 52 weeks a year.
2 Looking for low fares & quality service?
3 Last minute offers.
4 All of this at discount rates.
5 Delicious meals prepared by top-class chefs.
6 An incredible choice of ten music channels and the very latest movies.
7 Travelling to Moscow or St Petersburg?

4 Complete the sentences with words from the box.

before	at	for	like	on	only	with	to

1 We offer you unbeatable choice _____ unbeatable value.
2 You'll be in Poland _____ you know it.
3 _____ any good travel operator, we also offer a variety of additional services.
4 Our service is second _____ none.
5 You can rely _____ us to make your journey a memorable experience.
6 Our friendly and professional staff will be _____ too pleased to help.
7 Whether you're travelling on business or _____ pleasure, this is the choice for you.
8 _____ prices starting at £150, you won't find a better deal.

Check your answers in the advertisement for MillanAir.

WRITING

1 You are going to write an advertisement for MillanTours Coach Travel. Below is the first paragraph. Insert the missing words.

Poland is only a click away with MillanTours Coach Travel

MillanTours now offers three departures a week from London Victoria six top destinations in Poland (Warsaw, Krakow, Gdansk, Katowice, Poznan Wroclaw). When you arrive, we can help you hotel bookings and we can arrange connections to than 50 other destinations. With journey time of thirty hours between London Warsaw (including the regular rest stops), is no better or more convenient way to travel.

2 You are going to complete the advertisement in exercise 1. Decide in which order you want to use the information below.

- onboard video
- panoramic windows
- toilet and washroom facilities
- one way £60, return £100
- hotel bookings
- travel insurance
- air conditioning
- light snacks, hot and cold drinks served

- no extra charges
- onboard telephone
- non-smoking
- access for disabled passengers
- easy internet booking system
- money back guarantee

3 Write the rest of the advertisement. Use the points below to help you.

1 Is your information organized in a logical way?
2 Have you used an interesting variety of adjectives?
3 Are there any phrases in Language focus exercise 4 that you could use in your advertisement?
4 Look at all the nouns in your advertisement and check that you have used articles where they are needed.
5 Check your spelling and punctuation.

6 | An extract from a holiday brochure

ST LUCIA –
WHERE YOU DON'T HAVE TO DREAM

1

Our exclusive hotel, *The Coconut Club*, is situated near Marigot Bay, on the west coast, only a short drive from Castries. Set in 70 acres of palm trees and with stunning views of the bay, *The Coconut Club* offers excellent facilities. The hotel has its own private beach, as well as two swimming pools and a gym. (1) ___ If you enjoy food as well as (or instead of) sport, there are two superb restaurants, one of which serves traditional local dishes like Callaloo soup or Creole curry. (2) ___ Although you probably won't want to leave the hotel, it's only a short walk to the bars and restaurants in the village of Marigot Bay. For a special night out, The Shack, for example, is one of the most memorable restaurants in the area.

2

When you feel like a day away from the beach, it's easy to find activities for all the family. (3) ___ Take your pick from our huge range of excursions, including pony rides through the banana plantations, a morning at the breathtaking Diamond Waterfalls and a cruise around the island's fishing villages.

(4) ___ If you're looking for an action-packed holiday, you won't be disappointed either. With dozens of sports to choose from (windsurfing, mountain-biking, water-skiing and rock-climbing, for instance), there is sure to be something for you.

3

Located between Martinique and St Vincent, St Lucia is one of the Caribbean's best-kept secrets. With its beautiful white beaches, its tropical rainforests and its dramatic volcanic mountains, St Lucia's stunning beauty is everything you would expect of a Caribbean island. (5) ___ In the many pretty villages and towns, such as the picturesque capital, Castries, the islanders' warm welcome makes St Lucia the perfect holiday destination. (6) ___

READING

1 Read the extract from a holiday brochure and match the paragraphs 1–3 to the headings a–c.

☐ a The island
☐ b The resort
☐ c Things to do

2 Read the extract again and insert sentences a–f in the spaces 1–6.

a A trip to the weekly market in the capital will be a must for all your holiday souvenirs.
b In addition to tennis and squash courts, *The Coconut Club* also has a brand-new health spa.
c In fact, the only problem is that you won't have enough time to do everything that we offer.
d It is nothing less than a dream come true.
e The hotel's own beach bar also offers light snacks and drinks.
f Unlike many of its neighbours, the island has not been ruined by tourism.

3 Read the extract again and match the adjectives 1–7 to the nouns a–g.

1	our exclusive	a	capital
2	stunning	b	facilities
3	excellent	c	hotel
4	superb	d	restaurants
5	the breathtaking	e	views
6	pretty	f	villages
7	the picturesque	g	waterfalls

Read the extract again to check your answers.

LANGUAGE FOCUS

1 Insert a missing apostrophe in each of the extracts from the tourist brochure. Use the notes in the box to help you.

> 1 Put the possessive apostrophe before the *s* with singular nouns.
>   *The **hotel's** private beach has its own bar.*
> 2 Put the possessive apostrophe after the *s* with plural nouns.
>   *It's impossible to forget the **mountains'** beauty.*
> **NB** *its* = possessive form of *it*
>   *it's* = short form of *it is* or *it has*

1 Although you probably won't want to leave the hotel, its only a short walk to the bars and restaurants in the village of Marigot Bay.

2 When you feel like a day away from the beach, its easy to find activities for all the family.

3 Take your pick from our huge range of excursions, including pony rides through the banana plantations, a morning at the breathtaking Diamond Waterfalls and a cruise around the islands fishing villages.

4 Located between Martinique and St Vincent, St Lucia is one of the Caribbeans best-kept secrets.

5 In the many pretty villages and towns, such as the picturesque capital, Castries, the islanders warm welcome makes St Lucia the perfect holiday destination.

Read the extract again to check your answer.

2 Look at the extract again and underline examples of the language in the box.

X is	situated located	near … not far from …
	on the north/south/east/west coast.	
	set in …	
	a short drive from/walk to …	

3 Use the language in exercise 2 to write five sentences about a beach resort that you know.

4 Complete the sentences with words or phrases from the box.

for example   including   like

1 There are two restaurants, one of which serves local dishes _____ Callaloo soup.

2 The Shack, _____, is one of the most memorable restaurants in the area.

3 Take your pick from our range of excursions, _____ pony rides through the banana plantations or a morning at the Diamond Waterfalls.

Read the text again to check your answers.

WRITING

1 Use the notes to write an extract from a tourist brochure. Use the points below to help you.

maui Sunrise Hotel, maui

Maui - biggest island in Hawaiian chain / middle of Pacific Ocean / volcanic island / tropical forests / long sandy beaches / cosmopolitan resorts (eg Kapalua and Makena)

Hotel: The Maui Sunrise / Four-star / close to beach / west coast / views of ocean / golf course, tennis centre, swimming pool, two restaurants, two bars and nightclub / relaxed but elegant

Haleakala National Park, home of the biggest dormant volcano in the world / mountain bike down volcano at sunrise / go whale-watching / take a helicopter tour / walk the streets of the old capital Lahaina / wide range of water sports: kayaking, sailing, windsurfing

Remember to …
- present the information in a logical order.
- think how you're going to describe the location of the island and the hotel – have you used an interesting variety of adjectives?
- use the language in Language focus exercise 4 to help give you examples of the points you make.
- check your spelling, punctuation and use of capital letters.

7 | A letter of advice

READING

1 Emma sent the email below to the problem page of a website. What difficult decision does she have to make?

1 whether or not to accept a place at university
2 which university to go to
3 whether to continue living at home with her parents

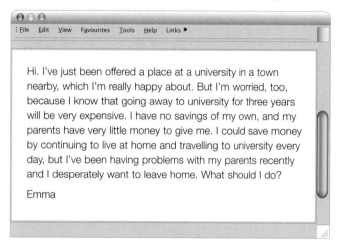

Hi. I've just been offered a place at a university in a town nearby, which I'm really happy about. But I'm worried, too, because I know that going away to university for three years will be very expensive. I have no savings of my own, and my parents have very little money to give me. I could save money by continuing to live at home and travelling to university every day, but I've been having problems with my parents recently and I desperately want to leave home. What should I do?

Emma

2 Emma got three replies to her email. Read the replies and decide which you think, 1–3, offers the best advice.

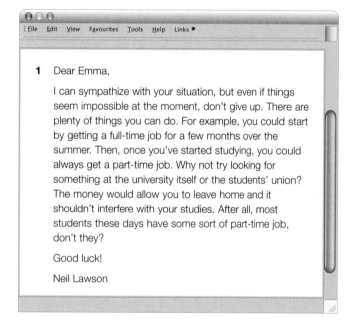

1 Dear Emma,

I can sympathize with your situation, but even if things seem impossible at the moment, don't give up. There are plenty of things you can do. For example, you could start by getting a full-time job for a few months over the summer. Then, once you've started studying, you could always get a part-time job. Why not try looking for something at the university itself or the students' union? The money would allow you to leave home and it shouldn't interfere with your studies. After all, most students these days have some sort of part-time job, don't they?

Good luck!

Neil Lawson

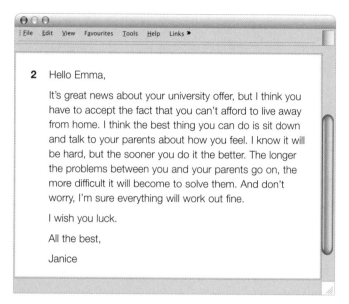

2 Hello Emma,

It's great news about your university offer, but I think you have to accept the fact that you can't afford to live away from home. I think the best thing you can do is sit down and talk to your parents about how you feel. I know it will be hard, but the sooner you do it the better. The longer the problems between you and your parents go on, the more difficult it will become to solve them. And don't worry, I'm sure everything will work out fine.

I wish you luck.

All the best,

Janice

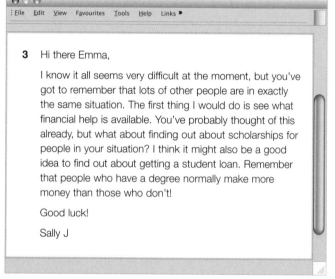

3 Hi there Emma,

I know it all seems very difficult at the moment, but you've got to remember that lots of other people are in exactly the same situation. The first thing I would do is see what financial help is available. You've probably thought of this already, but what about finding out about scholarships for people in your situation? I think it might also be a good idea to find out about getting a student loan. Remember that people who have a degree normally make more money than those who don't!

Good luck!

Sally J

LANGUAGE FOCUS

1 Find and correct the mistakes in the sentences. Check your answers in the emails in Reading exercise 2.

1 You could start by get a full-time job for a few months.
2 You could always getting a part-time job.
3 Why not to try looking for something at the university itself or the students' union?
4 I think the best thing can you do is sit down and talk to your parents.
5 The first thing I would do is seeing what financial help is available.
6 You've probably thought of this already, but what about find out about scholarships?

2 Rewrite these sentences using the words given.

1 If I were you, I'd stay at home.
The best thing *you can do is stay at home.*

2 Have you thought about taking out a student loan?
I think it might _____.

3 I think you should talk to your parents.
Why _____?

4 Have you tried finding a part-time job?
The first _____.

5 What you need to do is speak to a financial advisor.
Why not _____?

6 There's no harm in asking about scholarships.
You could start _____.

3 Rearrange the words in the phrases.

1 sympathize   your   can   situation   I   with .
_____

2 seems   know   all   I   difficult   very   it .
_____

3 luck   wish   you   I .
_____

4 give   don't   up !
_____

5 best   the   all .
_____

6 everything   work   I'm   sure   will   out   fine .
_____

4 Which phrases are …

a offering encouragement?
b closing the letter?
c expressing sympathy?

WRITING

1 Read two more emails that were sent to the same problem page. Match the advice 1–4 to the emails A and B.

A

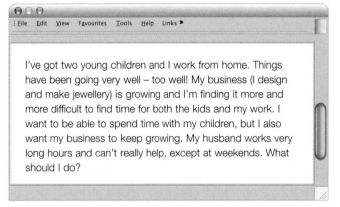

I've got two young children and I work from home. Things have been going very well – too well! My business (I design and make jewellery) is growing and I'm finding it more and more difficult to find time for both the kids and my work. I want to be able to spend time with my children, but I also want my business to keep growing. My husband works very long hours and can't really help, except at weekends. What should I do?

B

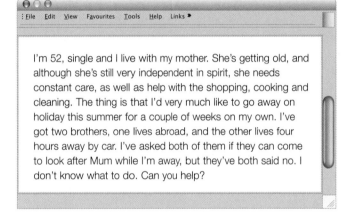

I'm 52, single and I live with my mother. She's getting old, and although she's still very independent in spirit, she needs constant care, as well as help with the shopping, cooking and cleaning. The thing is that I'd very much like to go away on holiday this summer for a couple of weeks on my own. I've got two brothers, one lives abroad, and the other lives four hours away by car. I've asked both of them if they can come to look after Mum while I'm away, but they've both said no. I don't know what to do. Can you help?

1 Ask your brothers if she can come and stay with one of them. ___
2 Find a childminder to help you out at home. ___
3 Book a holiday where you can both go and be independent of each other. ___
4 Concentrate on your business during the weekend. ___

2 You are going to write a reply to one of the two emails. Use the points below to help you.

1 Decide which email you're going to reply to.
2 Decide which piece of advice in exercise 1 you think is the best.
3 Think of a second piece of advice to include.

3 Write the email. Use the checklist below to help you.

1 Have you used a variety of expressions from Language focus exercises 1 and 2 to offer advice?
2 Have you opened your email with an expression of sympathy?
3 Have you closed it appropriately?
4 Check your spelling, punctuation and use of capital letters.

8 | A funny crime story

READING

1 Read the newspaper story and choose the best headline 1–4.

1 **Police arrest thieves outside police station**

2 **Thief makes good impression on girlfriend**

3 **VALUABLE CAMERA STOLEN**

4 **Thieves leave evidence on film**

Earlier this month, the police in St Trudy, in north-west England, found a stolen car with a camera in *it*. When the film was developed, Detective Inspector Anderson found herself looking at pictures of the
5 thieves. 'I couldn't believe it,' she said, but, as a result of the discovery, the thieves were quickly arrested.

The extraordinary story had begun the previous day when out-of-work engineer, Bill Madison, met Sandy Jason. Madison wanted to make a good
10 impression on her, so he stole a brand new Ford Mondeo to take *her* out on a date. Neither of them had much money and *they* therefore decided to spend the evening driving around town.

While Ms Jason was looking through the glove
15 compartment of the car, she found a camera, and so she decided to use *it* to take pictures of her boyfriend in action. The pictures included one of *him* happily driving the wrong way down a one-way street. Later in the evening, they ran out of petrol and, because
20 they had no money, decided to abandon the car. They left *it* in a no-parking zone near a police station. Consequently it was found almost immediately.

Because of their hurry to leave the scene of the crime, they completely forgot about the camera.
25 Madison was found guilty of theft, but the judge decided that Ms Jason was innocent after she said that she had no idea the car was stolen.

2 Read the story again. Put the events in the correct order.

- [ ] He stole a car.
- [ ] He took her out on a date.
- [ ] Bill Madison met Sandy Jason.
- [ ] Sandy took photos of Bill.
- [ ] The police arrested Bill and Sandy.
- [ ] The police developed the film in the camera.
- [ ] They abandoned the car.
- [ ] They ran out of petrol.

LANGUAGE FOCUS

1 Look at the different ways that we can use linkers to show the result of an action.

> He lost his job, **and so/so** he was short of money.
> He lost his job. **As a result/Consequently/Because of this/Therefore**, he was short of money.
> He lost his job. He was **therefore/consequently** short of money.
> He was short of money **as a result of** losing his job.
> He was short of money **because** he had lost his job.

Find and underline these expressions in the story.

2 Choose the best word or phrase to complete the sentences.

1 Madison wanted to impress his girlfriend. He *as a result of / therefore* needed a car.
2 Madison didn't have a car, *because / so* he stole one.
3 They abandoned the car *consequently / because* they ran out of petrol.
4 The police officer knew the man in the picture and he was *as a result / therefore* arrested immediately.
5 The judge believed Ms Jason's story. *Because / Consequently* he decided that she was innocent.
6 *As a result of / Therefore* Ms Jason's experience, she decided to end her relationship with Madison.

3 Look at the pronouns in bold italics in the story. Who or what do they refer to? The line numbers are in brackets.

1 it (2) _____
2 her (11) _____
3 they (12) _____
4 it (16) _____
5 him (17) _____
6 it (21) _____

4 Read the story and replace the words in italics with pronouns.

Angie worked in a large bookshop in Oxford. One day, *Angie* was chatting to the store detective when *Angie* saw a man in a wheelchair who was trying to get into the store. There was a step outside the shop and *the man* couldn't get his wheelchair over the step. *Angie* went over to help *the man with the wheelchair* but *the wheelchair* was too heavy, so Angie asked the store detective to help, too. Together, *Angie and the store detective* helped the man into the shop. When *Angie, the store detective and the man in the wheelchair* were all in the shop, Angie returned to the cash desk. *Angie* thought that there was something strange about the man and *Angie* therefore decided to watch *the man*.

Writing

1 The pictures below continue the story from Language focus exercise 4. Decide which order the pictures should go in and use your imagination to decide what happened next.

2 Write the story. Use the points below to help you.

1 Organize your writing into logical paragraphs.
2 Remember to include descriptions of the people and places in the story.
3 Have you used all the past tenses (past simple, past continuous and past perfect)?
4 Try to use time expressions or linkers of result to show the connections between different events.
5 Try to use a variety of ways to refer to people in the story.
6 Remember to check your spelling and punctuation.

9 | A letter of complaint

READING

1 Read the letter of complaint. What is the writer complaining about?

a a delivery has been lost in the post
b there has been a mistake with a delivery
c a delivery is taking a long time to arrive

---

(1) *Dear Sir/Madam,*

(2) *I am writing to complain about* your online delivery service which (3) *has failed to deliver* three books and two DVDs I ordered two months ago (on April 14).

Last week I sent an email to your online customer service department and (4) *I was informed that* the order would arrive in three weeks. However, (5) *I am afraid this is totally unacceptable.* I am particularly disappointed because the books were supposed to be a birthday present for my husband and although I ordered them well in advance, they will not arrive in time for his birthday.

(6) *To resolve the problem* I would like (7) *a full and immediate refund.* The purchase number is JB607 8932. If I do not hear from you within the next five days, (8) *I shall be forced to* contact my solicitor. (9) *Please contact me* by email or by phone on 01296 54327.

(10) *I look forward to hearing from you* and to a quick resolution of this problem.

(11) *Yours faithfully,*

LANGUAGE FOCUS

1 Match the information 1–4 to the descriptions a–d.

1	Sarah Philips	a	date
2	Attn: Customer Care Manager	b	writer's address
3	34, Old Kent Rd, Canterbury, CN5 4SL	c	writer's name
4	June 15 2006	d	title of the person you're writing to

2 In which paragraph (1–3) does the writer ...

a explain the problem? ___
b say what she wants the company to do? ___
c explain why she's writing? ___
d say what she'll do if the problem is not solved? ___

3 Write the number of the formal phrases in italics in the letter next to the informal equivalents below.

a to sort things out _6_
b it isn't good enough ___
c I'm not happy about ___
d they told me that ___
e All the best ___
f still hasn't sent me ___
g Hi there ___
h I hope to hear from you soon ___
i you can get in touch with me ___
j my money back now ___
k I'm going to have to ___

4 Read the information in the box.

We use *although* and *however* to contrast two pieces of information.

We use *although* to join the two pieces of information in one sentence.

Although *I ordered them in advance, they will not arrive in time.*

We use *however* to show the connection between two sentences.

I was informed that the order would arrive in three weeks. **However**, *I am afraid this is totally unacceptable.*

When we use *however* at the beginning of a sentence, it is always followed by a comma.

---

5 Delete the three sentences that are grammatically incorrect.

1 Although I placed my order two months ago, it has still not arrived.
2 However I placed my order two months ago, it has still not arrived.
3 I placed my order two months ago, however it has still not arrived.
4 I placed my order two months ago. However, it has still not arrived.
5 I placed my order two months ago. It has still not arrived, however.
6 My order has still not arrived. Although, I placed it two months ago.

6 Connect the pairs of sentences using the word in brackets.

1 They guarantee same-day delivery. The flowers arrived three days late. (*although*)
2 The flowers finally arrived. They were sent to the wrong address. (*however*)
3 Mum was very disappointed. She saw the funny side of it. (*although*)
4 I had never used the company before. Friends had told me that they were very good. (*however*)

WRITING

1 Read the email below. What is the problem?

1 They delivered the wrong flowers.
2 They delivered the flowers to the wrong address.
3 They delivered the flowers on the wrong day to the wrong address.

Hi Phil,

How are you doing? Have you spoken to Mum recently? Has she told you about the flowers? I wanted to send her some flowers for Mother's Day, so I ordered some online at Lightning Deliveries. Have you ever used them? I hadn't, but I'd heard they were pretty good. On the website they promised to deliver them on the same day – but they got there three days late! I mean, what's the point of sending flowers on Mother's Day if they don't get there on the right day? And to make matters even worse, they got the address wrong and sent them next door. At least Mum's got a sense of humour. I think she was a bit disappointed not to get anything on Mother's Day, but she laughed about it when Tom from next door turned up with a bouquet of roses for her! But it was a bit expensive for a joke. I'm going to write to complain. I don't see why I should pay for flowers that were delivered late and to the wrong person! I'll let you know what happens.

Love,

Sarah

2 You are Sarah. You are going to write a letter of complaint to Lightning Deliveries. Look at the email in exercise 1 again and make notes about what you're going to say in the paragraph plan below.

1 why you are writing
2 what exactly happened
3 what you want the company to do and what will happen if the problem is not solved

3 Write the letter. Remember to include your address, the title of the person you're writing to and the date.

4 Look at what you have written. Can you improve it in any way? Use the points below to help you.

1 Have you used appropriate expressions to open and close the letter?
2 Is your letter formal enough?
3 Have you used linking expressions to show the connection between what you expected and what actually happened?
4 Check your spelling and your use of punctuation and capital letters.

NB We do not use contractions in formal language.

10 | A narrative

READING

1 Read the story and put the paragraphs in the correct order.

☐ Being absolutely fanatical about bullfighting, Templar always went to Spain for his holidays. His hairdressing salon was covered in bullfighting posters and he shared his passion with his customers. 'He always asked how you were and talked about the weather,' said one customer, 'but you knew that, within a few minutes, the subject would change to bullfighting.'

☐ But that year, Templar did not return. At first, no one was worried about him, thinking that he had decided to stay in Spain. He had often said that he wanted to live there. After a while, however, his family began to suspect that something had happened to him. They began to make their own enquiries and, before long, they discovered that he had not got onto his plane or checked into his hotel. They contacted the police at once. An investigation was launched, but Templar was never seen again. Finding no trace of him after ten years, the police eventually pronounced him dead.

☐ It was only after the announcement of Templar's death in July 2004 that his disappearance became really mysterious. Later that month, the head of a British anti-bullfighting organization received a letter from Shirley Sheard, Templar's lawyer, saying that he had left him £250,000 in his will. Templar had written this new will on the day before he vanished.

☐ On July 10 1993, hairdresser Gavin Templar left his shop in Bury, Lancashire with a sign in the window which said he would be back on July 21. Seeing the sign, regular customers were not surprised because they knew that Templar always took his summer holidays in July.

2 Read the story again and answer the questions.

1 What do you think happened to Templar?
2 Why do you think that Templar changed his will?

LANGUAGE FOCUS

1 Correct ten spelling mistakes in the paragraph below.

Templar's family were absolutly determined to find an explanation for his mysteryous disapearance. They knew that he had appeared woried in the days before he closed the shop. Continuing their enquiries, they eventualy discovered that the head of the anti-bullfighting organization had been a custemer in Templar's shop. When they recieved information that this man had the same name as Templar's laywer, they knew they were close to discoverring the truth. But, by then, it was already too late. Shirley Sheard and her husband had vannished.

Read the story again and check your answers.

2 Complete the paragraph with words from the box.

after	at	before	later	that	within

It was a day that would change Gavin Templar's life.
(1) _____ morning, he had told a customer about his plans to buy a house in Spain.
(2) _____ long, the conversation had turned to bullfighting and (3) _____ a few minutes of meeting the two were arguing. (4) _____ that afternoon, the customer returned to the shop and threatened him. Templar tried to ignore him, but, (5) _____ a while, the man pulled out a knife and said he would be back. Templar called his lawyer for advice. She told him to close the shop (6) _____ once and come to see her.

3 Read the information in the box.

We can combine two sentences that have the same subject with a present participle.
Regular customers saw the sign. They were not surprised.
Seeing *the sign, regular customers were not surprised.*
They found no trace of him. They pronounced him dead.
Finding *no trace of him, they pronounced him dead.*

4 Combine the pairs of sentences with a present participle.

1 He was thinking about his plans to buy a new house. He was in a good mood.
2 He was feeling frightened. He called his lawyer.
3 He closed the shop. He went to see his lawyer.
4 The customer sat down in the chair. He asked Templar about the posters on the walls.
5 The family discovered the man's name. They knew they were close to the truth.
6 The Sheards knew they were in trouble. They decided to disappear.

WRITING

1 Match the pictures 1–5 to the notes a–e.

☐ a beautiful day / cool swimming pool / Monica dives into pool / finds dead fish / panics / must have killed it!
☐ b Monica very happy / large, beautiful house / big garden / note on fridge / lots of food
☐ c finds fish shop / happy to find same type of fish as dead one / buys new fish / hopes family will not notice
☐ d hot day / June / Wilson family in a hurry / plane to catch / taxi arrives / Monica looking after Wilson family house
☐ e family comes home / good holiday / happy and suntanned / go to garden / see fish / horrified / scream

2 Use the notes and the pictures to write the story. Use the checklist below to help you.

1 Have you used all the past tenses (past simple, past continuous and past perfect)?
2 Use time expressions to show the connections between the different events.
3 Try to combine some sentences with a present participle.
4 Look at all the nouns and check your use of articles.
5 Check your spelling and punctuation.

3 Some stories have a 'twist' where something unexpected happens at the end. Read the 'twist'.

> Monica was back home when the phone rang.
> 'Hello?' she said.
> 'It's Mrs Wilson,' said the voice at the other end.
> 'Thank you for looking after the house. However, there is a little problem.'
> Monica panicked. Did they know about the fish? 'Oh, really?' she said. 'What's that?'
> 'Well, when we went on holiday, I forgot to tell you that the fish in the swimming pool was dead. And now it's swimming around again!'

READING

1 Read the information page about the London Marathon. Match the headings a–d to the paragraphs 1–4.

☐ a The sporting event   ☐ b History   ☐ c Spectators   ☐ d How to take part

THE **LONDON** MARATHON

1

The race was founded by former Olympic® runner and sports journalist Chris Brasher. Chris had taken part in the 1979 New York Marathon and was inspired by his experience. On his return to the UK, he began speaking to politicians and private companies in order that London, too, could become the setting of a world-class marathon. Within two years, Brasher realized his dream and in the first year 7,747 athletes took part in the race. Twenty-five years later, it has become one of the top events in the athletics calendar and raises millions of pounds for charity each year.

2

The London Marathon is one of Britain's greatest annual events. It is held in April every year and is more of a party than a race. It attracts more than 40,000 competitors and, for the top runners, it is a race of world importance. But most of the runners take part in order to raise money for charities and the atmosphere is more one of fun and solidarity than of serious competition.

3

The London Marathon receives many more applications than there are places for runners and application forms must be completed before the end of October. Full details are available on the official website www.london-marathon.co.uk where spectators can also get information about the race route and a list of pubs that support the event.

4

Anyone who has seen the race will tell you that it is an incredible sight. Every year, literally millions of spectators line the streets, and many will take their places early in the morning so as to get the best places to watch. The runners come in all shapes and sizes. Many wear strange and colourful costumes so that they can be recognized by their friends and supporters, who are ready to provide refreshments along the way. Dozens of celebrity runners also add to the atmosphere of fun.

2 Read the information page again and tick the information which is mentioned.

1 The amount of money that has been raised for charities in the last ten years.
2 The month of the year when the race happens.
3 The name of last year's winner.
4 The name of the founder of the marathon.
5 The names of celebrities that take part.
6 The number of participants in the first race.
7 The reason why most runners take part in the race.
8 The way to find out where to watch the race.

LANGUAGE FOCUS

1 Read the information in the box.

> We can use *in order to, so as to* and *so that* to show the reasons for an action.
>
> Use *in order to/so as to* + infinitive.
>
> *Most of the runners take part **in order to** raise money for charities.*
>
> Use *in order that/so that* + clause.
>
> *Many wear strange costumes **so that** they can be recognized by their friends.*

2 Choose the best way to complete the sentences.

1 Brasher went to Boston *so as to* / *so that* he could learn more about the organization of marathons.
2 Applications must be sent in early *in order that* / *in order to* be considered.
3 Runners should train for many months *so as to* / *so that* be fit enough to take part.
4 Central London streets are closed *in order that* / *in order to* runners do not have problems with the traffic.

3 Read the information in the box.

> a Use commas between clauses in long sentences in order to make them easier to read. A comma in writing represents a short pause in speech.
> b Use commas between items in lists, except for the last two items when we use *and* or *or*.
> c Use commas to introduce direct speech.
> d Use commas after the thousands when you are writing numbers. (Many other languages use a full stop.)

4 Match the examples 1–4 to the rules a–d in exercise 3.

☐ 1 More than 40,000 competitors take part.
☐ 2 The competitors include runners, walkers, skaters and stilt artists.
☐ 3 More than 70% of the participants are amateurs, many first-time marathon runners, running to raise money for charity.
☐ 4 As one organizer explained, 'We encourage anybody and everybody to take part.'

5 Add the missing commas to the description.

> The New York City Marathon is one of the world's greatest marathons attracting more than 85000 applicants. The prize money is more than $500000 but many athletes take part because they will be watched by over 2000000 spectators. As in all modern day marathons the runners also include charity fund raisers fun runners and amateurs looking for that once-in-a-lifetime experience. As veteran runner Mark P says 'Crossing the finish line in Central Park was the greatest thrill of my life.'

6 Complete the sentences in column A with the phrases in column B.

A

1 ___ is one of the country's greatest annual events.
2 It is held every year in ___.
3 The event attracts more than ___.
4 Every year, thousands of people ___.
5 ___ also add to the atmosphere.
6 The best place to watch is ___.

B

a 200,000 people
b from one of the bridges
c line the river to watch
d March or April
e Special events in pubs, food stalls and souvenir sellers
f The University Boat Race

7 Think of an important sporting event in your country and complete the sentences 1–6 in exercise 6.

WRITING

1 Use the four headings in Reading exercise 1 to make notes about either a local or national sporting event in your country.

2 Write an information page about the event. If you are not sure about precise or interesting details, feel free to use your imagination. Alternatively, you could research on the internet.

3 Read what you have written. Can you improve it in any way? Use the points below to help you.

1 Have you included enough interesting details about the event and its history?
2 Have you described the atmosphere?
3 Have you used any phrases from the page about the London Marathon to help you?
4 Check your spelling and punctuation.

12 | Writing a report

READING

1 Read the opening section of a report and supply the missing figures 1–4 in the table below.

The UK Family Spending Survey

Introduction

Over 5,000 families took part in this survey. The data was collected over a period of twelve months from February 2005 to January 2006. (1) *The results of the survey were released on May 25.* This report presents the main results of this annual survey into the nation's spending habits.

1   General Trends

This section of the report will look at how much money an average family spends, what they spend it on and how their spending changes (2) *with age.*

1.1 Average weekly spending

(3) *The survey shows that* the average British family spends £453 a week. They spend more on transport than anything else, with an average of £65 per week. Leisure time activities come next with families spending an average of £59 a week on TVs, computers, newspapers, books, cultural and sports activities and package holidays. Food and drink come third,

while health and education come at the bottom of the list. Average spending on health is £6.20 a week and £6 on education.

1.2 How spending varies with age

(4) *The results also show* how spending varies with age. People aged 30 to 45 spend the most, an average of £564 a week, while people aged 70 or over spend the least, with an average of £187. The amount of money people spend on food and non-alcoholic drinks increases with age. People under 30 spend only seven per cent of their money on food and drink, while people aged 70 or more spend seventeen per cent. However, (5) *the same is not true* when it comes to eating out. (6) *The money spent* on restaurants decreases with age. (7) *The under 30s* spend ten per cent of their money on restaurants and hotels, while (8) *those aged 70 or over* only spend five per cent.

The UK Family Spending Survey 2005–2006: family spending

Average weekly spending

Total spending including:	£453
Transport	£65
Leisure time activities	(1) _____
Food and drink	£44
Education	£6.20
Health	(2) _____

Variations with age

Age:	under (3) ___s	over (4) ___s
Food & drink	7%	17%
Restaurants & hotels	10%	5%

2 Read the report again and decide if the sentences are true (T) or false (F). Correct the false sentences.

1   The survey is held once a year. ___
2   The report compares family spending and income. ___
3   People generally spend more on food and drink than they do on sport and other free time activities. ___
4   People do not generally spend a lot of money on education. ___
5   Older people generally spend much less than younger people. ___
6   Older people generally spend less on food and drink than younger people. ___

LANGUAGE FOCUS

1 Match the number of the phrases in italics 1–8 in the report to the phrases a–h.

- ☒ a   people who are over 70
- ☐ b   in this survey we can see that
- ☐ c   people who are under 30
- ☐ d   they gave out the results on May 25
- ☐ e   according to how old they are
- ☐ f   from the results we can see
- ☐ g   the amount of money people spend
- ☐ h   things are different

2 Rearrange the words to make sentences. Check your answers in the report.

1 family   £453   British   spends   the   week   a   average .

_____

2 transport   spend   more   anything   they   than   on   else .

_____

3 bottom   health   of   come   the   at   list   the   and   education .

_____

4 30   to   45   most   the   spend   people   aged .

_____

5 money   amount   the   spend   on   food   increases   with   of   people   age .

_____

WRITING

1 Look at the tables and answer the questions.

The UK Family Spending Survey 2005–2006: children's spending

Number of children surveyed: 10,000
Data collected between May 2005 and January 2006.

Table 1: General breakdown of expenditure for children aged 7–16

	Girls	Boys	All
Total weekly spending including:	£13.60	£12.40	£13.00
sweets & snacks	£2.60	£2.40	£2.50
other food	£2.30	£2.50	£2.40
clothes & shoes	£2.90	£1.10	£2.00
toys, hobbies & pets	£0.40	£2.00	£1.20
games, music & DVDs	£0.90	£2.20	£1.60

Table 2: Examples of significant variations (age & gender)

	7–11		12–16	
	Girls	Boys	Girls	Boys
Total expenditure including:	£7.20	£6.80	£21.50	£20.40
sweets & snacks	£2.30	£2.50	£6.50	£7.20
games, toys, hobbies & pets	£1.40	£2.80	£0.50	£2.40

1 How many children were interviewed for the survey?
2 When did the survey take place?
3 How much do children spend a week on average?
4 Who spend more on average, girls or boys?
5 Which age group spends the most?
6 Which age group spends the most money on sweets and snacks?
7 Which age group spends the most money on games and toys?
8 What do girls spend the most on? And boys?

2 You are going to write a report on children's spending habits. Look at the plan and your answers to the questions in exercise 1. Decide what information you are going to include in each section.

1 Introduction
2 General summary
3 Breakdown of specific information
4 Conclusion

3 Write the report. Use the checklist below to help you.

1 Present the information in a logical progression from general to specific.
2 Choose relevant expressions from Language focus exercises 1 and 2.
3 Refer to the figures in the tables in exercise 1.
4 Check your spelling and punctuation.
5 Use decimal points when writing the amounts of money.

Useful language to improve your writing

Language for describing

Describing people
He gives the impression of being ...
She's really keen on ...
He's really good at ...
Her most prominent feature is ...

Describing towns & cities
One of the most popular places with visitors is ...
Other interesting historical landmarks include ...
When the weather is good, why not ... ?
A must for all visitors is the ...
For people looking for a night out, there is/are ...

Discussion language

Advantages & disadvantages
There are a lot of advantages to ...
For a start, ...
For example, ...
Secondly, ...
The most important reason for ... is ...
However, there are some disadvantages, too.
First of all, ...
What is more, ...
Finally, ...
To sum up, ...

Narrative language
First of all ... .
Initially ... .
Eventually ... .
In the end ... .
Before long, ...
After a few minutes, ...
Later that afternoon, ...
After a while, ...
Seeing the sign, regular customers were not surprised.
Finding no trace of him, they pronounced him dead.

Advertising language

Advertising a service
We offer you unbeatable choice ... .
Our service is second to none.
Our friendly and professional staff will be only too pleased
  to help.
You can rely on us to make this a memorable experience
  for you.
With prices starting at £10, you won't find a better deal.
All of this at discount rates.
We never forget you have a choice.

Advertising a holiday
X is situated near ...
X is located not far from ...
X is on the west/east/south/north coast.
X is set in ...
X is a short drive from/to ...

Language for giving advice
Have you thought about ... ?
I think you should ...
Why don't you ... ?
Have you tried ... ?
There's no harm in ...
You could start by ...
If I were you, I'd ...

Language for giving results
As a result, ...
Consequently, ...
Therefore, ...
He was short of money *as a result of* losing his job.
He was short of money *because* he had lost his job.

Language for complaining
I am writing to complain about ...
I am afraid this is totally unacceptable.
I am particularly disappointed because ...
Although I ordered them well in advance, they will not
  arrive in time.
I was informed the order would arrive three weeks late.
  However, this is totally unacceptable.
To resolve the problem I would like to request a full and
  immediate refund.
If I do not hear from you within the next five days, I will
  be forced to contact my solicitor.

Language for explaining
Most runners take part *in order to* raise money for charity.
Many of the runners wear strange costumes *so that* they
  can be recognized by their friends.
Runners train for many months *so as to* be fit enough to
  take part.
Central London streets are closed *in order that* runners do
  not have problems with the traffic.

Report language
The survey is held once a year/once every two years ...
The report compares ... and ...
People generally spend more on ...
People do not generally spend a lot of money on ...
Older people generally spend much less than younger
  people (on) ...
The same is not true of ...
The money spent on ... decreases/increases with age.
The under 30s/over 40s tend to spend more on ...
The results show ...

Irregular verbs

Infinitive	Past simple	Past participle
be	was/were	been
beat	beat	beaten
become	became	become
begin	began	begun
bend	bent	bent
bite	bit	bitten
blow	blew	blown
break	broke	broken
bring	brought	brought
build	built	built
burn	burned/burnt	burned/burnt
burst	burst	burst
buy	bought	bought
can	could	could
catch	caught	caught
choose	chose	chosen
come	came	come
cost	cost	cost
cut	cut	cut
deal	dealt	dealt
do	did	done
draw	drew	drawn
dream	dreamed/dreamt	dreamed/dreamt
drink	drank	drunk
drive	drove	driven
eat	ate	eaten
fall	fell	fallen
feed	fed	fed
feel	felt	felt
fight	fought	fought
find	found	found
fly	flew	flown
forget	forgot	forgotten
forgive	forgave	forgiven
freeze	froze	frozen
get	got	got
give	gave	given
go	went	gone
grow	grew	grown
hang	hanged/hung	hanged/hung
have	had	had
hear	heard	heard
hide	hid	hidden
hit	hit	hit
hold	held	held
hurt	hurt	hurt
keep	kept	kept
kneel	knelt	knelt
know	knew	known
lead	led	led
learn	learned/learnt	learned/learnt
leave	left	left
lend	lent	lent
let	let	let

Infinitive	Past simple	Past participle
make	made	made
meet	met	met
pay	paid	paid
put	put	put
read	read	read
ride	rode	ridden
run	ran	run
say	said	said
see	saw	seen
sell	sold	sold
send	sent	sent
shut	shut	shut
sit	sat	sat
smell	smelt	smelt
speak	spoke	spoken
spend	spent	spent
stand	stood	stood
steal	stole	stolen
swim	swam	swum
take	took	taken
tell	told	told
win	won	won

Meet me in Istanbul

1 Journey to Istanbul

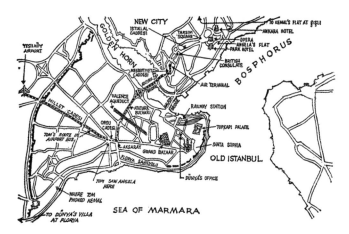

It is early morning on a sunny spring day in April. Heathrow Airport, London, is busy, as usual. Hundreds of people are arriving, leaving, or waiting for planes.

In the Departure Lounge of Terminal One, a man is sitting reading a newspaper. He does not like airports. There are too many people, and he is always nervous when he flies. He looks at his watch impatiently. Then he hears the announcement over the loudspeakers.

'British Airways announce the departure of Flight BE570 for Istanbul. Will passengers please proceed to Gate 16 for boarding.'

Tom Smith picks up his suitcase and walks towards Gate 16.

Twenty minutes later, the plane is preparing to leave. It moves slowly across the airport to runway number two. Tom is sitting looking out of the window.

The plane suddenly moves forward, races down the runway and rises into the air. Tom looks down at the houses and roads far below, and smiles. London is behind him. Now he is on his way to Istanbul.

Tom relaxed and took a letter from his pocket.

Resat Bey Apt 11–3,
Kamerot Sokak,
Ayazpasa, Istanbul

My dear Tom,

Thank you for your letter. I am so happy that you can come and visit me for a holiday. Life here in Istanbul is very interesting. I am enjoying my work, but I miss you very much. It will be wonderful to see you again.

I'm sure we will have a very nice holiday. Spring is here, and the weather is beautiful.

I have to work on Monday 14th of April – the day you arrive. So I can't come to the airport to meet you, but you can take a taxi from the Air Terminal to Taksim Square. That's in the centre of the new part of the city. There's a big hotel called the Park Hotel near the square. I'll meet you there at 5 o'clock. We'll meet in the American Bar. The view over the city is beautiful.

I can't wait to see you again, Tom. I have so much to tell you. So remember, the Park Hotel, Taksim Square, 5 o'clock.

See you on the 14th.

Love,

Angela.

Tom sat for a moment, looking at his fiancée's letter. Then he put it in his pocket. He looked down at the green fields of France, as the plane continued its journey across Europe.

'Have you been to Istanbul before?' said a voice. It was the young man in the next seat.

'No, I haven't,' said Tom. 'Have you?'

The man smiled.

'My home is in Istanbul. I'm studying in London at the moment. I'm going home for a holiday.'

'Really?' said Tom. 'Where are you studying?'

'At London University.'

The two men sat talking, as the stewardesses began serving lunch. The young man told Tom his name was Kemal. His parents had a shop in Istanbul.

'Are you meeting someone in Istanbul?' Kemal asked.

'My fiancée,' said Tom. 'She's working in Istanbul.'

'That's interesting. How long has she been there?'

'She went to Istanbul two months ago. She works for a small company which is starting to export to England. She's making all the arrangements.'

'Exporting always seems so difficult,' said Kemal.

'It seems difficult,' Tom agreed. 'But that's Angela's job. She's an expert in importing and exporting. Her father has an import/export agency in London and she has worked for him for some years. She's almost completed her work in Istanbul now. The company has already started to send goods to England. She'll be coming back to London soon.'

'What kind of goods do they export?' asked Kemal.

'All kind of things – brass ornaments, coffee-pots, trays, leather and onyx articles – Angela's father thinks these goods will sell very well in England.'

'That's interesting,' said Kemal. 'My parents sell things like that in their shop in Istanbul.'

The two men went on talking as the plane flew over Italy and Greece towards Turkey. Soon they were descending to Yesilkoy Airport, Istanbul.

When the plane stopped, Kemal stood up.

'I hope you enjoy your stay in Istanbul,' he said. 'Here's my telephone number. If you need anything, phone me. I live in Sisli. It's not far from the centre of the city.'

'Thanks, Kemal, that's very kind of you.'

'Not at all,' replied Kemal. 'Nice to meet you. And now, goodbye.'

Tom went through Customs and Immigration and walked towards the airport exit.

A bus for the City Air Terminal was waiting outside the airport. Tom got in and sat down beside the window. Other passengers got on and the bus left the airport and drove towards Istanbul.

Soon they were driving past the houses and apartment blocks near the city. Then they passed the old city walls. Tom felt excited, and looked at everything. He saw beautiful old mosques and street markets.

The bus was now approaching the centre of old Istanbul. It stopped at some traffic lights.

A car stopped beside the bus. The door opened and a woman got out. Two men were with her. Suddenly Tom jumped to his feet. It was Angela!

'Angela!' Tom shouted. 'Angela! Here! It's me, Tom!'

He knocked on the bus window. Suddenly the traffic lights changed and the bus moved forward. Tom ran to the back of the bus. Angela and the two men were going into a building.

'Angela!' he shouted. 'An . . . ' He stopped. It was too late. The bus was moving quickly down a wide street. The passengers were looking at Tom and he suddenly felt foolish. He walked back to his seat and sat down.

Suddenly Tom jumped to his feet. It was Angela!

What a surprise, he thought to himself. I must tell her when I see her this evening.

Then the bus crossed Ataturk Bridge and Tom looked at the boats on the Golden Horn. Again he felt excited.

The bus arrived at the Air Terminal at a quarter to four. There were some taxis waiting there. Tom went up to one.

'The Park Hotel, Taksim Square, please,' he told the driver.

'English? You come with me. I take you quickly.'

At a quarter past four, the taxi arrived in the square.

'Here you are, sir, the Park Hotel.'

'Thank you,' said Tom, and paid the driver.

Tom went into the hotel. He found the American Bar and sat down at a table on the terrace. A waiter came out.

'A beer, please,' said Tom.

He sat in the afternoon sunshine, and looked down over the city of Istanbul. The view was very beautiful. He was looking at the sea. The Bosphorus was full of ships. There were very big ships going to Russia and little sailing ships. In the distance, he could see the mosques and palaces of old Istanbul. How beautiful and how exciting!

Tom looked at his watch. It was nearly five o'clock. He got up and walked up to the hotel entrance. There were lots of people going in and out of the hotel. But he did not see Angela anywhere. He went back to the bar and ordered another beer.

Come on Angela, Tom said to himself. Don't be late.

Just inside the American Bar a man in a grey raincoat was sitting at a table. He was drinking coffee and smoking cheap cigarettes. A newspaper lay open on the table in front of him, and from time to time he looked at it. But the man wasn't reading the newspaper – he was watching Tom.

It was now twenty past five. Tom sat in the evening sunshine. He looked at his watch again, and waited. Half past five. Quarter to six. It was getting dark. He looked at the lights on the Bosphorus. Strange, thought Tom. Angela isn't usually late.

Tom sat at the table, on the terrace of the American Bar, waiting for his fiancée. He waited, and waited, and nobody came.

And the man in the grey raincoat sat patiently inside the bar, smoking, and watching Tom.

'Another beer, sir?' asked the waiter.

'No, bring me a black coffee, please. Have you a telephone?'

'Yes, sir, inside.'

Tom went into the hotel. There was a telephone beside the reception. Tom dialled Angela's number. The phone rang and rang, but nobody answered it. He put the phone down and turned towards the reception desk.

'Excuse me,' he asked the receptionist, 'Kamerot Sokak – do you know where it is?'

'Yes, it's very near. Go out of the hotel entrance and turn right. Walk along the street – and Kamerot Sokak is fourth on the right.'

'Thank you,' said Tom.

Tom went back to the bar. He drank his coffee and paid for his drinks. It was now after eight o'clock. Tom picked up his suitcase and left the hotel.

Inside the bar, the man in the grey raincoat stood up and picked up his newspaper. He put some money on the table and walked out into the street. He stood on the pavement for a moment or two, then started walking.

Kamerot Sokak was a narrow, quiet street of old apartment buildings. Tom walked along the pavement, looking at the numbers on the doors. There was only one street light and it was difficult to see. But finally, he found Angela's address, number 11.

The building had a large glass door. Tom pushed it, but it was locked. There was no bell. He knocked on the door. Nothing happened. He knocked again, louder this time, and listened. Silence.

Damn, he thought. He was impatient now. And worried.

He stood back in the middle of the street and looked up. There were five floors, and all the windows were black. There was no light anywhere in the building.

Angela, he said to himself, Angela! Where are you?

A short distance away, the man in the grey raincoat stood in a dark doorway. He was watching Tom, watching every move he made . . .

Tom did not know what to do. He knocked once more on the glass door – again nothing happened. Finally, he picked up his suitcase. With a last look at the building, he turned and started walking back towards Taksim Square.

Tom Smith, he thought to himself, as he walked. You need a hot bath and a good sleep. Then you can decide what to do.

The Park Hotel was expensive, but Tom remembered seeing one or two small hotels near Taksim Square. Finally, he was standing outside the Ankara Hotel. He went in.

'Good evening,' he said to the woman at reception. 'I'd like a single room, please.'

The woman nodded.

'We have a nice room upstairs. Come, I'll show you.'

They went upstairs and she opened a door.

'Very nice room,' she said.

It was small, but it was clean and it looked comfortable.

'I'll take it,' he said, and gave the woman his passport.

'The bathroom is along the corridor,' she said. 'Breakfast is from eight to ten o'clock. Goodnight.'

Tom put his case down and sat on the bed. He suddenly felt very tired and unhappy. He was not having a good dinner in a nice restaurant. He was not sitting with the woman he loved. He was sitting alone, in a cheap hotel, in a strange city.

For a long time he sat on the bed thinking, But I saw Angela. I saw her from the bus!

Finally he stood up.

OK, he thought. Tomorrow morning I'll go to Angela's office and find out what has happened. There's a very simple explanation, I'm sure. I'll find out tomorrow.

He had a hot bath and got into bed. He was very tired after his long journey and soon fell asleep.

The man in the grey raincoat walked across Taksim Square. There was a telephone kiosk in the corner. He dialled a number, and waited. Then he spoke.

'He's in the Ankara Hotel,' the man said. 'He waited at the Park Hotel and then he went to the girl's flat. Now he's in the Ankara Hotel . . . Yes, yes, of course I will.'

He put down the phone and left the kiosk.

The next morning, Tom felt much better. He had breakfast, then took a taxi to the office where Angela worked.

The taxi drove through the busy streets and crossed the Galata Bridge into the old city. Finally, it turned into a small street near the Railway Station. It was a narrow street of shops, small businesses and workshops. The taxi stopped in front of a grey building.

"F. Karamian and Co. Export/Import Agency", said the sign above the door. Tom pushed open the door and went in. A secretary was typing at the reception desk. She looked up as Tom came in.

'Good morning,' she smiled.

'Good morning,' said Tom. 'My name's Tom Smith. I'm looking for Angela Thomson – she's my fiancée. I arrived in Istanbul last night and waited for her, but she didn't . . .'

The secretary was staring at him. She stood up.

'Wait a moment, please, Mr Smith.'

She hurried over to a door marked "Office", and went inside. Tom could hear her talking to someone.

The door opened and a man came out. He looked very serious.

'Mr Smith, my name's Dünya. Please come in.'

Tom went into the office.

'Please sit down, Mr Smith,' said Dünya. 'Look – er, I don't know how to tell you this, Mr Smith. I have some very bad news for you. I'm very sorry indeed, but Miss Thomson, your fiancée – is – is dead.'

Drink this, Mr Smith,' said Mr Dünya. He handed Tom a glass of strong brandy. Tom sat, shocked, white-faced, unable to speak. He drank the brandy slowly.

'How – how did it happen?' he asked.

'A car accident. Miss Thomson was driving along a dangerous road. No one knows what happened. Her car went off the road and fell down the hillside.'

'Yesterday evening?' Tom asked.

'I beg your pardon?'

'The accident – it happened yesterday evening?'

Dünya looked at him.

'Mr Smith, the accident happened a week ago – last Sunday to be exact. She had been away to Bursa for the weekend and . . .'

'But that's impossible!' said Tom. 'I saw Angela yesterday!'

'Yesterday?'

'Yes. I was on the airport bus, coming into Istanbul. I saw her in the street.'

'I'm terribly sorry, Mr Smith, but you're making a mistake.'

'No, I tell you I saw her. I . . .'

'Mr Smith,' Dünya said patiently, 'Istanbul is a big city. There must be hundreds of women here who look like your fiancée.'

Tom said nothing.

'The British Consulate were very helpful,' continued Mr Dünya. 'They made all the arrangements for the funeral. It was on Wednesday.'

'Have her parents been told about this?' Tom asked.

'That is a problem, I'm afraid. Her parents are on holiday in France. The British and French police are trying to contact them.'

'So they don't know yet,' said Tom quietly.

'No, they don't, I'm afraid.'

There was a long silence.

'Can I have another brandy, please?' asked Tom.

'Of course.'

Tom tried hard to think clearly.

'I thought I saw her yesterday,' he said softly.

'I understand, Mr Smith. It's a great shock – a terrible tragedy for you – for all of us.'

After a pause, Dünya asked, 'What will you do now, Mr Smith? Is there anything I can do to help?'

'I'm not sure,' said Tom. 'I need some time to think. I don't know what to do.'

'Do you know anyone in Istanbul?'

Suddenly Tom remembered Kemal.

'Yes, yes, I have friends, don't worry. Look, Mr Dünya, I can't decide anything now. I think I'll stay in Istanbul for a day or two. I'd like to visit the Consulate, and maybe the police.'

Mr Dünya opened a drawer in his desk and took out a card. He wrote on it and handed the card to Tom.

'I've written down the telephone number of Mr David Pennington. He's the man in the Consulate who made the arrangements for the funeral. The other number is my office telephone number. Contact me if you need anything. I'm here during the day.'

Tom stood up.

'I must go now,' he said. 'Thank you, you've been most kind.'

Mr Dünya walked with him to the door. 'Well, Mr Smith, once again, I'm terribly sorry.'

'You know I was so sure I saw her. So sure . . .' Tom said.

'I understand,' replied Dünya. 'It's a terrible shock.'

The two men shook hands.

'Remember, come here any time if you need anything,' said Mr Dünya. 'Goodbye, now.'

'Goodbye,' said Tom, and walked out into the street.

Mr Dünya turned and walked back into his office. He closed the door carefully and sat down at his desk. For a few minutes he sat thinking. Then he picked up the telephone.

Tom walked slowly through the crowded streets of old Istanbul. The streets were busy, and full of interesting people, shops and cafés. But Tom did not see any of those things. He was not interested in Istanbul, he was not a tourist any more. Tom was thinking of Angela. He remembered the journey on the bus from the airport. He was sure he had seen Angela. She had been there on the pavement, getting out of a car. But Dünya said it was not Angela. Angela was dead. She had died a week ago.

Tom walked through the streets of the city. He walked through the Grand Bazaar. He walked on and on through narrow old streets. He didn't know where he was, or what time it was. He thought about Angela. He thought again about his journey on the bus from the airport. Again and again he thought about it, and again and again he saw his fiancée. Then he stopped walking, and stood for a moment on the pavement. He was standing on a street beside the sea.

Angela isn't dead, he thought. I saw her!

He looked in his pocket and found Kemal's telephone number. He walked quickly across the street to a café. He went inside to the telephone.

'Hello, Kemal? Hello, it's me, Tom. Remember . . .? Yes, yes, fine thanks. Listen, remember you said I could phone you if I needed anything? Well, something has happened. Can we meet somewhere?'

So,' said Kemal, 'you really think you saw her, do you?' Kemal and Tom were sitting in the American Bar at the Park Hotel. Tom thought carefully for a moment before answering.

'Yes,' he said slowly. 'Yes, I do. You probably think I imagined it. I understand that. But I'm convinced I saw her, that's all.'

Kemal nodded.

'I can't stop thinking about yesterday,' Tom continued. 'I close my eyes and I can see Angela there on the pavement. I can't forget that.'

'Listen, Tom,' said Kemal. 'We only met yesterday but already we're friends. You're in my country, you're my friend, and you need help. If you think you saw Angela, that's enough for me. I believe you. Now we have to decide what to do.'

'There are two things I want to do as soon as possible,' said Tom. 'I want to go to the street where I saw Angela. Then I want to go to the British Consulate. I have an appointment[27] for this afternoon.'

'OK,' said Kemal. 'The street where you saw Angela. Do you think you can remember where it is?'

'No problem,' said Tom. 'We can drive along the same route as the airport bus. I'm sure I'll remember it.'

'And what do you think you will find there?'

'I'm not sure. But she was going into a building with two men. At least we can find the building – maybe that will tell us something.'

'OK,' said Kemal. 'My car's outside. Let's go.'

Tom and Kemal were driving through the city.

'It was a wide street,' said Tom. 'We came to a roundabout after the traffic lights. We turned left and then we passed an old aqueduct.'

'Aksaray,' said Kemal. 'It's near here.'

Kemal drove over Ataturk Bridge. After a few minutes, they saw the old aqueduct. Then they came to a large roundabout and turned right.

'This is it,' said Tom. 'It's somewhere near here.'

They were approaching some traffic lights. Tom looked out of the window at the buildings on the left.

'No,' he said. 'Not here.'

They drove on to the next traffic lights.

'This is it,' said Tom. 'This is the place.'

Kemal stopped the car.

'You get out. I'll find a parking place.'

Tom got out and looked around him. He was in a wide street of shops and offices. A newspaper kiosk, a travel agency – he remembered them from the day before. He stood looking at the buildings opposite until Kemal arrived.

Tom pointed across the street to the entrance to an office building.

'That's it, I think,' he said.

They crossed the street and looked at the name plate beside the entrance to the office block. There were many names there a lawyer, a dentist, a doctor, and many other offices. Tom stood looking at the names for a few moments.

'Well,' he said finally, 'I'm sure she went into this building. But which office was she going to? Was she going to see a lawyer, or a dentist, or a doctor? How do we begin to find out?' Kemal took his arm gently, and they walked slowly back to the car.

'Listen, Tom,' he said. 'You're going too fast. You can't expect to find out everything immediately. Wait until you see the man at the Consulate. After that, we'll think about it. Then we can decide what to do. We know she was going into that building. That's something, anyway. Now look, it's lunch-time. You must be hungry. I know a good restaurant near here …'

'You're right,' said Tom. 'We have to be patient.'

After lunch, Kemal drove Tom to the British Consulate in Mesrutiyet Street. He stopped the car at the gate.

'Well, good luck,' he said. 'I'll wait for you.'

Tom opened the car door.

'It's very good of you to help me like this Kemal. Thanks very much.'

'Not at all,' said Kemal. 'See you later.'

Tom went through the Consulate gates. The old Consulate, with beautiful gardens round it, looked like a palace. Tom pushed the big door open and went in.

'I'd like to see Mr David Pennington, please,' he said at the reception desk. 'My name's Tom Smith. I have an appointment.'

After a few minutes, a tall man wearing glasses came to meet him.

'Mr Smith, my name's Pennington. How do you do?' said the man, holding out his hand.

Tom shook Mr Pennington's hand. 'How do you do,' he replied.

'Come into my office, please, Mr Smith. Mr Dünya told me you were coming.'

They walked up the beautiful staircase of the Consulate and went into Mr Pennington's office.

'Sit down, please,' said Pennington. 'Mr Smith, I'm very sorry about your fiancée. It was a great tragedy. Please accept my condolences.'

'Thank you,' said Tom.

Mr Pennington took two files from his desk.

'This is our report on the accident,' he said. 'And this is the police report. I can give you copies of these, but perhaps you'd like to ask me some questions first.'

Tom thought for a moment.

'Mr Pennington,' he said, 'I think I saw Angela yesterday.'

Pennington stared at Tom. There was silence in the room. Pennington looked down at his desk, then he looked at Tom again. Tom was able to hear the noise of the traffic in the street outside the gardens. For a long time Pennington said nothing. At last he spoke.

'Mr Smith,' he said, 'I don't think you fully understand. Your fiancée …'

'I know,' Tom interrupted. 'Angela was killed in a road accident last weekend. Her funeral was last Wednesday. Mr Dünya told me that this morning. But I'm telling you I saw her yesterday.'

'Mr Smith, I think you should read these reports carefully before you say anything more.'

He passed the files over to Tom.

'Can I get you a cup of tea or something?'

'A cup of tea would be nice. Thank you.'

Pennington left the office. He came back a few minutes later with some tea. There was silence in the room while Tom read the reports. Presently he looked up.

'After the accident,' Tom asked Pennington, 'how did they identify the body?'

'That was difficult,' said Pennington. 'As you know, the accident happened on a dangerous road about 200 kilometres from here. Your fiancée's car crashed through a wall by the side of the road, and fell down the hillside. The car burst into flames and was completely burned out. The – the body was very badly burned, so identification was difficult. But the police found your fiancée's handbag lying near the car. Her passport and papers were in the handbag. The police found out that the car was owned by a car hire company. Miss Thomson had hired the car for the weekend.'

'What about Angela's parents?' Tom asked.

'I'm afraid her parents don't know about the accident yet. They're on a camping holiday in France – the police are trying to contact them.'

'What was she doing on that dangerous road?'

'She spent the weekend in Bursa, sightseeing. It's a very interesting old town. She was on her way back to Istanbul.'

Tom thought for a moment.

'And are the police quite satisfied?' Tom asked.

'Yes,' said Pennington. 'The police are convinced that it was an accident. The file is closed.'

'And you people at the Consulate,' said Tom quietly, 'are you satisfied?'

For a moment Pennington said nothing.

'Yes, Mr Smith, we are,' he said. 'Our job, among other things, is to look after British citizens in Turkey. We have looked into this matter very carefully. And we are satisfied that it was an accident.'

Tom said nothing.

'I really am very sorry,' Pennington went on. 'I understand how you must feel. You've had a terrible shock. My advice to you now is to leave Istanbul. There is nothing you can do here.'

'I'm beginning to think you're right,' said Tom. 'Perhaps I should go home. You know, I really thought I saw Angela, but now . . .'

'Where are you staying?' asked Pennington.

'The Ankara Hotel, near Taksim Square.'

'Will you be all right? Do you know anyone here?'

'I'm all right, thank you. I have a friend here.'

'Well Mr Smith, please think carefully about what I've said. I hope you'll take my advice. If you need anything before you leave, contact me. I'll be glad to help you.'

'Thank you,' said Tom, standing up. 'Thank you for all you've done.'

'Not at all,' said Pennington. 'I'm sorry your visit to Istanbul wasn't a happier one. Have a good journey home. Goodbye.'

The two men shook hands and Tom left the Consulate.

Kemal was waiting in the car outside the Consulate gates. 'What did he say?' Kemal asked, as Tom got in the car.

'The same as Dünya,' Tom replied. 'It was an accident. Angela's dead. The file is closed.'

Kemal started the car, and drove away from the Consulate.

'Mr Pennington advised me to go back to London,' Tom continued. 'I'm beginning to think he's right.'

Kemal said nothing.

'The police think Angela is dead, and the people at the Consulate do too. I'm the only person who doesn't think she's dead. So what am I going to do? Stay here in Istanbul? Go home? Really, I just don't . . .'

'Now wait a minute, wait a minute, Tom,' said Kemal. 'How long have you been in Istanbul?'

'Not very long . . .'

'You've been here less than twenty-four hours. And what has happened to you in this time? You've had a terrible shock. You've been told that your fiancée was killed in an accident a week ago. But you are sure you saw her from the bus last night. So now you are confused and you don't know what to do. That's right, isn't it?'

Tom nodded his head slowly in agreement.

'Well, I'll tell you what you're going to do,' Kemal went on. 'You're going to come with me to the Topkapi Palace. We can walk through the beautiful gardens there and think about everything carefully. Then we can decide what to do next.'

Tom smiled.

'You're right, of course. It has been a difficult day.'

'Exactly,' said Kemal. 'Now it's time to relax a little.'

They were driving down narrow streets, to the Golden Horn.

'This is the Galata Bridge – it crosses the Golden Horn,' said Kemal. 'Look, isn't it beautiful?'

They drove slowly across the bridge in the bright sunlight.

'It is beautiful,' said Tom, looking out across the Bosphorus. 'Very beautiful.'

They continued across the bridge, turned left, and drove past the Railway Station. A few minutes later they came to Santa Sophia – one of the oldest and most beautiful buildings in Istanbul. It was once a church, then a mosque and now it is a museum.

'We'll leave the car here,' said Kemal. 'First, I'm going to show you the Palace of Topkapi.'

They got out of the car in a large park. They were standing in front of the first gate of the Palace.

'The Sultans of Turkey used to live in Topkapi Palace,' Kemal explained.

Kemal and Tom bought an entrance ticket. They walked through the gate into the gardens of the Palace.

'This is the first courtyard of the Palace,' went on Kemal. 'Over there are the royal kitchens. And over there the harem – that's part of the Palace where the women lived.'

They were walking down a wide path. Kemal looked round and then he took Tom by the arm.

'Walk a little faster,' he said quietly.

Tom saw that there was a strange look on Kemal's face.

'Is anything wrong?' he asked.

'Keep walking,' said Kemal. 'And don't look back.'

They walked across the courtyard towards the second gate of the Palace.

'Kemal, what's wrong?' said Tom quickly.

'Someone is following us,' answered Kemal.

'Someone following us?' said Tom. 'What do you mean?'

'There's a man in a grey raincoat walking behind us. I saw him when we came into the Palace. I wasn't sure at first, but I am sure now.'

They walked on and then ran through the second gateway. Kemal looked back. The man was still following them.

'This way. Quickly.' Kemal led Tom to the entrance of the Treasury. Inside, it was very crowded and it was also dark after the bright sunshine.

'We're going to separate now,' said Kemal. 'The man won't be able to follow both of us. You take a taxi back to your hotel. Have you got some money?'

'Yes,' said Tom.

'Right, I'll phone you this evening.'

'What are you going to do?' asked Tom.

'I'm going back to my car.'

'Be careful,' said Tom.

'You too,' said Kemal. 'See you later.'

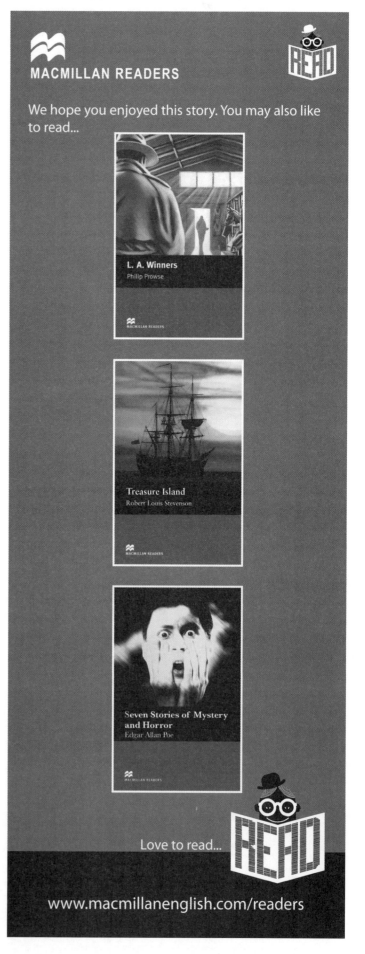

Answer key

1A Double lives

Stative & dynamic verbs

1 1 don't believe   2 is thinking   3 want
4 likes   5 is costing   6 hate

2 Do you believe; do you know; you love; It asks; you are thinking; you want

Vocabulary from the lesson

3 1 by a member of your family   2 sincere
3 ahead someone   4 honesty   5 about a story

4 1 liar   2 great   3 nervous   4 date
5 sweaty   6 fidgeting

Dictation

5 💿 **01**
1 Do you ever lie about why you are late?
2 She seems to be telling a lie.
3 Stop fidgeting and tell me the truth.
4 He's looking for a new job at the moment.
5 We think he's lying about his age.
6 They appear to be completely sincere.

💿 Read & listen

6 💿 **02** Refer to the reading text *Liars!* on page 6 of the Student's Book.

1B Daily lives

Present simple & present continuous

1 1 am interviewing   2 are doing   3 lives
4 works   5 make   6 like   7 has
8 get   9 am doing   10 are you enjoying

Verbs with two meanings

2 1 am thinking/'m thinking   2 don't think
3 have   4 am seeing/'m seeing   5 see
6 is having/'s having

Translation

3 Translate the sentences into your language. Check with your teacher.

1C Britishness

Subject & object questions

1 1 b   2 c   3 b   4 a   5 a   6 a
Subject questions: 1, 2, 4.
Object questions: 3, 5, 6.

2 1 wrote   2 belong   3 stand   4 live   5 won
6 women hold

3 1 f   2 c   3 a   4 e   5 b   6 d

4 1 What frightens you?
2 Who is your favourite British writer?
3 Where do you live?
4 Which party did you vote for?

Self-image

5 1 c   2 e   3 a   4 g   5 b   6 f   7 d

Dictation

6 💿 **03**
1 I would describe myself as calm and organized.
2 If anybody asked, I would say I am a Londoner and a European.
3 What happened to people's interest in politics?
4 How many people speak two languages in Britain?
5 I don't see myself as British, but I'm proud to be English.
6 Do you know anyone who thinks this test is a good idea?

1D First impressions

Describing people

1 1 What does he look like   2 muscular   3 pale
4 prominent   5 straight   6 what's his hair like
7 shaved   8 blond   9 eyes

2 Picture B

3 1 shaved   2 wide   3 healthy
4 blond   5 prominent   6 slim

4 1 like   2 like   3 looks
4 look as if   5 looks like   6 looks

Translation

5 Translate the sentences into your language. Check with your teacher.

1 Reading

1 1 c   2 b   3 a   4 c   5 c
2 1 c   2 d   3 e   4 a   5 b   6 f

💿 Read & listen

3 💿 **04** Refer to Reading 1 *You never get a second chance to make a first impression* on page 8.

2A Around the world

Vocabulary from the lesson

1 1 trip   2 travels   3 travel   4 adventure
5 hitchhiked   6 journey

Present perfect & past simple

2 The story started; He realized; Boorman immediately agreed; they experienced; they had; has been a real success

3 1 have/'ve (just) got back
2 did (you) get back   3 landed   4 had
5 have (you) been   6 went
7 have met/'ve met   8 did (you) meet
9 got married   10 did (you) get married

Dictation

4 💿 **05**
1 I remember I spent eight months in Egypt as a child.
2 The programme took a fascinating look at animals in America.
3 Has he travelled around Europe on his own?
4 We didn't arrive in Amsterdam until almost eight o'clock.
5 I've never eaten Indian food in England that's as good as in India.
6 The film is an interesting account of a family travelling around Africa.

💿 Read & listen

5 💿 **06** Refer to the reading text *Lawyer gives up job to cycle around the world* on page 16 of the Student's Book.

2B Unusual journeys

Phrasal verbs

1 1 out   2 across   3 over   4 off   5 up   6 off

2 1 saw (me) off   2 came across   3 picked (me) up
4 dropped (me) off   5 has sorted (it) out   6 has got over

3 1 Did you get over your illness in a hospital?
2 The villagers offered to look after my motorbike.
3 Could you drop us off in Paris, please?
4 I came across an old school friend in a tea house in Darjeeling, India.
5 We sorted out a lift to La Paz in Bolivia.
6 The doctor's family looked after me when I got malaria in Pakistan.

Translation

4 Translate the dialogue into your language. Check with your teacher.

2c Down under

Present perfect for unfinished time

1 1 got   2 have visited/'ve visited
3 had   4 has been/'s been   5 was
6 have never seen/'ve never seen
7 left   8 have been/'ve been

2 1 last week   2 during the last two weeks
3 up till now   4 over the last two months
5 since 1990   6 recently

Vocabulary from the lesson

3 1 popular destination
2 so many things to see and do
3 cultural and historical
4 best-known monuments
5 landmark
6 settle down

Dictation

4 💿 **07**
A: How long have you been in Krakow?
B: Only three days. We arrived last Saturday.
A: Oh, really! And what have you done up to now?
B: Lots. We haven't stopped in the last three days.
A: Have you seen the Royal Castle?
B: Yes. We walked up to it yesterday afternoon.
A: Oh, good. And have you been to the Market Square yet?
B: Yes, I love it.

2D Getting around

Travelling

1 1 A single to the airport, please.
2 Could you tell me the time of the next train to Bristol, please?
3 Have you got change for a five-pound note, please?
4 Could you tell me when we get to York Road, please?
5 I'd like a cab for Dorset Road in Ealing, please.
6 Can I get a taxi anywhere around here?

2 *Sample answers:*
1 Could you tell me the time of the next train to Plymouth, please?
2 I'd like a cab for Picadilly Circus, please.
3 Have you got change for a five-pound note, please?
4 A first-class return ticket to Manchester, please.
5 Can I get a taxi anywhere around here?
6 Could you tell me when we get to Church Road, please?

Verb collocations (travel)

3 1 catch   2 missed   3 get off   4 took   5 drop
6 walk   7 take   8 arrived

Translation

4 Translate the sentences into your language. Check with your teacher.

2 Reading

1 2 ✓   3 ✓   6 ✓   7 ✓   8 ✓

2 1 F (Eddie usually performs to large audiences.)
2 F (Eddie has made a number of Hollywood films.)
3 T
4 F (Eddie spent five weeks training to be ready to run the marathons.)
5 T
6 F (Eddie ran marathons in Scotland.)
7 F (Eddie has decided to do more tough endurance events.)

3 1 talented   2 huge   3 tough   4 not bad
5 headed   6 pointed out

💿 Read & listen

4 💿 **08** Refer to Reading 2 *Eddie Izzard – the marathon man!* on page 13.

3A Dream homes

Modals of obligation, permission & prohibition (present time)

1 Person a – 1;   Person b – 2;
Person c – 2;   Person d – 1

2 1 don't need to   2 aren't allowed to   3 don't need to
4 can't   5 can   6 can   7 don't have to   8 have to

Dictation

3 💿 **09**
1 Do the people who rent have to do any housework?
2 You aren't allowed to keep pets in the house.
3 Do I need to pay a deposit for the flat?
4 Residents don't have to pay any gas or electricity bills.
5 You mustn't put out any rubbish before eight.

4 🔘 **10** Refer to the reading text *Paradise Ridge* on page 27 of the Student's Book.

3B Unusual homes

Vocabulary from the lesson

1 1 facilities   2 local   3 share
4 accommodation   5 move   6 detached

Accommodation

2 1 holiday home   2 rented accommodation
3 suburbs   4 flat   5 apartment block
6 terraced house   7 mobile home   8 tree house

Make, let & allow

3 1 let   2 allows   3 allow   4 make
5 let   6 let   7 let   8 make

Translation

4 Translate the sentences into your language. Check with your teacher.

3C Bedrooms

Verb collocations (sleep)

1 1 fall   2 get   3 set   4 wake   5 nap   6 feel

Modals of obligation, permission & prohibition (past time)

2 1 had to   2 didn't need to/didn't have to
3 weren't allowed to   4 could/were allowed to
5 didn't need to/didn't have to
6 could/were allowed to

3 1 had to   2 had to   3 had to   4 were allowed to
5 could   6 didn't have to   7 didn't need to

Vocabulary from the lesson

4 1 complain   2 sleepy   3 peace a chance
4 a disagreement   5 bed

Dictation

5 🔘 **11**
1 I didn't have to wear a school uniform when I was a child.
2 When I was sixteen I was allowed to stay out till midnight.
3 When my parents were in class at school they had to stand up when a teacher came in.
4 Last night I didn't need to do any homework, so I went to see a film.
5 In my grandfather's time, children were not allowed to speak until spoken to.

3D Dinner invitation

Requests

1 1 Can you   2 Can I   3 Would you mind
4 I wonder if I could   5 Would you mind if I
6 Could you

2 1 Can I use   2 Could you tell   3 if I close
4 I'm afraid you can't.   5 Do you think   6 if I go

3 1 P   2 D   3 P   4 P   5 D   6 P

Translation

4 Translate the dialogue into your language. Check with your teacher.

3 Reading

1 3

2 1 c   2 b   3 d   4 a

3 1 T
2 T
3 F (He rarely has problems with residents or the police.)
4 F (He thinks everyone has to do something.)
5 F ('WWOOFs' are not paid money for their work.)
6 T

4 1 a fixed abode   2 constraints   3 hassle
4 slashed   5 gigs   6 stuff

Read & listen

5 🔘 **12** Refer to Reading 3 on page 18.

4A Luck of the draw

Past simple & past continuous

1 1 won   2 crossed   3 was watching   4 bought
5 made   6 was listening   7 was living
8 was reading

2 1 told   2 shared   3 were talking   4 suggested
5 decided   6 were sitting   7 were having   8 had

Vocabulary from the lesson

3 1 a lot at stake   2 raise money   3 win the lottery
4 against the odds   5 scratchcards   6 charities
7 jackpot

Dictation

4 🔘 **13**
OK, I know it's against the odds, but every week millions play the lottery. I won once. I was sitting in a café having breakfast when the numbers came up on the radio. I thought I had all six. I jumped up and screamed 'I'm a millionaire!' But I wasn't. I had three numbers and won £57.

Read & listen

5 🔘 **14** Refer to the reading text *Lottery winners and losers* on page 36 of the Student's Book.

4B Twists of fate

Past perfect simple

1 2 1,2   3 2,1   4 2,1   5 2,1   6 1,2   7 1,2

2 1 went   2 had broken   3 had twisted   4 put
5 had left   6 skidded/had skidded   7 grabbed
8 entered/had entered   9 ignited   10 had been

Injuries

3 1 twisted/sprained   2 bruise   3 bleeding
4 suffering   5 unconscious   6 scratches
7 sprained/twisted   8 black eye

Dictation

4 💿 **15**

1 As soon as we received the call we went to rescue the man.
2 The hospital telephoned me because a bus had knocked down my brother.
3 She'd broken her leg three times by the age of ten.
4 When the police found her she'd been unconscious for three hours.

4c Bad luck stories

Time linkers

1 1 while   2 The moment   3 by the time   4 As soon as   5 As

2 While/As they were taking; When/The moment/As soon as they got back; By the time the police;

When/The moment/As soon as/As they threw away; while/when the staff; by the time he noticed

Vocabulary from the lesson

3 1 hung (her washing) out   2 cut off   3 got away   4 locked (him) out   5 jumped onto   6 put (her make-up) on

Translation

4 Translate the sentences into your language. Check with your teacher.

4d Fancy that!

Both & *neither*

1 1 both of us   2 We're both from Edinburgh   3 Neither did I   4 neither of us liked   5 Both of us are divorced   6 I do

2 1 Both superchap and ladybug
2 Both superchap and ladybug
3 Both superchap and ladybug
4 Neither superchap or ladybug
5 Only ladybug
6 Only superchap
7 Both superchap and ladybug
8 Only ladybug

Talking about similarities & differences

3 1 d   2 b   3 a   4 f   5 c   6 e

4 1 Neither didn't I.   2 So do I.   3 I too.   4 Neither I have.   5 So I am.   6 I can, too.

Translation

5 Translate the text into your language. Check with your teacher.

4 Reading

1 a 2   b 4   c 1   d 3

2 1 a   2 b   3 a   4 a   5 b   6 b   7 a

3 1 attend   2 attract   3 ordinary   4 headed to   5 complicated   6 chose   7 cheering   8 keen   9 at random

💿 **Read & listen**

4 💿 **16** Refer to Reading 4 *A win on the horses* on page 23.

5a Hard sell

Adjectives (advertising)

1 1 comfortable, fashionable, strong, stylish, popular
2 comfortable, efficient, popular, reliable, stylish
3 delicious, healthy, popular
4 comfortable, fashionable, stylish, popular
5 efficient, reliable, popular

2 1 comfortable   2 popular   3 stylish   4 reliable   5 efficient   6 fashionable

Comparisons 1

3 2 c   3 d   4 a   5 a   6 c   7 b   8 d

4 *Possible answers:*
1 The XTC Wave lasts longer than the OMD Cloud.
2 The OMD Cloud is heavier than the XTC Wave.
3 The XTC Wave is bigger than the OMD Cloud.
4 The OMD Cloud is smaller than the XTC Wave.
5 The XTC Wave is cheaper than the OMD Cloud.
6 The experts think the OMD Cloud is the best smartphone.

💿 **Dictation**

5 💿 **17**

1 Children are much bigger spenders now than ten years ago.
2 The Music Master is one of the best mp3 players on the market.
3 The Travelling Tunes mp3 is more expensive than the other one.
4 Sales of mobile phones to children are much higher than five years ago.
5 Children watch much less TV now.

💿 **Read & listen**

6 💿 **18** Refer to the reading text *Catch them young* on page 46 of the Student's Book.

5b Cold calling

Comparisons 2

1 2 fruitier than other cereal bars
3 different from other cereal bars
4 as healthy as *Super cereal* bars/healthier than *Super cereal* bars
5 more popular with children than other cereal bars
6 cheaper than *Super cereal* bars/as cheap as *Super cereal* bars

2 1 Branded trainers are often the same quality as normal trainers, but just more expensive.
2 I don't think that your mobile is as good as mine.
3 Yuck! That fizzy drink is not as good as *Koola Kola!*
4 That new digital camera isn't very different from the older version.
5 I think the new XP3 smartphone is much better than the XP2.
6 Why did you buy that DVD player? It's very similar to the one you already have.

Adjectives (negative prefixes)

3 **dis**: honest, satisfied; **un**: lucky, prepared, successful; **im**: patient, polite; **in**: accurate, correct, convenient, sufficient

4 1 inconvenient   2 unlucky   3 dishonest   4 impolite   5 dissatisfied   6 unprepared   7 impatient   8 unsuccessful

Translation

5 Translate the sentences into your language. Check with your teacher.

5c The office

Comparing nouns

1 1 most   2 longest   3 best   4 hardest   5 longer   6 most   7 more   8 quickest   9 less

Office activities

2 1 make; coffee   2 write; report   3 make; photocopies   4 emails, sent   5 received; call   6 make; phone calls

Vocabulary from the lesson

3 1 9 to 5   2 colleagues; boss   3 laptop; cell phone   4 at my desk   5 a staff   6 get some work experience

Dictation

4 🔲 **19**
1 I send and receive most of my email in the morning.
2 Do you have fewer holidays than your colleagues?
3 They always have more work to do on Friday.
4 She has less free time than I do.
5 Some workaholics spend more time in the office than at home.

Read & listen

5 🔲 **20** Refer to the reading text *Office Stereotypes* on page 50 of the Student's Book.

5d Paperwork

Office supplies

1 **horizontal:** paperclip, Post-it, Tipp-Ex, drawing pins, notepad
vertical: rubber, ink cartridge, Sellotape, pencil sharpener, highlighter

On the phone

2 1 Could I take a message
2 Could you tell him
3 Could you say that again
4 will he be back in the office
5 I don't think he'll be back until tomorrow morning
6 I'll call back then

3 Because the caller is very impolite.

4 **C:** <u>I want to</u> *Please could I* speak to Ms Horne.
S: Who's calling, please?
C: John Stratford from Stratford Cars.
S: I'm sorry, but Ms Horne's not at her desk. Would you like to leave a message?
C: Yes, please. <u>Tell her</u> *Could you ask her* to call me.
S: Excuse me!?
C: <u>Get her</u> *Could you ask her* to call me when she gets back, <u>OK</u> *please*?
S: Well … yes. Do you have a number?
C: <u>Yes</u> *Of course*. It's 0267 3416.
S: 0267 3416?
C: That's right.
S: I'll pass the message on.
C: <u>Good</u> *Thank you.*

Translation

5 Translate the telephone dialogue into your language. Check with your teacher.

5 Reading

1 1 c   2 d   3 e   4 a   5 b

2 1 c   2 b   3 c   4 b   5 b

4 1 takeaway and snack food   2 clothing and footwear, games, toys, hobbies, pets, music accessories   3 (2%)   4 boys   5 11%

6a Summer holiday

Future 1 (future plans)

1 1 are having   2 It'll be   3 we're seeing   4 we'll probably just get   5 going to have   6 I'll phone

2 I am seeing/I'm seeing my mother; I will see/I'll see you at Kate's; I am going to pick up/I'm going to pick up some brochures; he is going to be/he's going to be in Hong Kong; I'm sure you will enjoy/you'll enjoy it; Is Manuela coming

Holidays 1

3 1 picked up a brochure   2 chosen a destination   3 find your way around   4 pay a deposit   5 book the flights   6 do the packing

Dictation

4 🔲 **21**
1 I'll probably pick up some brochures from the travel agent's later.
2 We're going to book a last-minute holiday to France or Spain.
3 What are we going to do after we arrive at the resort?
4 The flight's leaving at six, so we need to check in at four thirty.
5 Are they going to stay at the hotel or will they leave tonight?

6b Getting away

Holidays 2

1 1 magnificent white beaches   2 cosmopolitan guests   3 exclusive, upmarket hotel   4 range of water sports   5 unforgettable beach parties   6 secluded beach   7 picturesque mountains   8 the beaten track   9 crowded beach parties   10 laid-back atmosphere

2 1 c   2 a   3 b   4 f   5 d   6 e

Future 2 (predictions)
3 1 will own/'ll own   2 is going to be/'s going to be
3 are going to miss/'re going to miss
4 will not pass/won't pass   5 will win
6 will break/'ll break

6c Perfect day

Present tenses in future time clauses
1 1 we'll take a studio tour   2 Once the tour is over
3 you'll visit some of the   4 you'll meet
5 You'll have a chance   6 before the coach leaves at six

Vocabulary from the lesson
2 1 rock-climb   2 drink   3 sightseeing
4 the packing   5 land   6 car

3 1 holiday makers   2 a taste of   3 guided tour of
4 feel in the mood   5 hire bikes

🔊 Dictation
4 🔊 22
1 As soon as you have arrived at the airport a travel rep will meet you.
2 The reception staff will be more than happy to take your bookings.
3 This historic town has two castles and a beautiful little harbour.
4 If you enjoy the trip to Dublin, you'll probably enjoy Cork, too.
5 When we receive your payment, we'll send you confirmation of the booking and a receipt.

🔊 Read & listen
5 🔊 23 Refer to the reading text *Emerald Tours* on page 60 of the Student's Book.

6d Travel plans

Indirect questions
1 1 ✓ 3 ✓ 5 ✓
2 ✗ I wonder if you could tell me if you have flights going from London, Heathrow to Vietnam?
4 ✗ Do you know how long the flight takes?
6 ✗ Could you tell me how much the flight costs, please?

2 1 I wonder if you could tell me if you have flights going from London, Heathrow to Vietnam
2 Do you know how long the flight takes
3 And can you tell me if that's a direct flight
4 Could you tell me how much the flight costs, please
5 Do you think you could tell me how much Business and Economy cost
6 I'd also like to know if I can book a hotel through you

Collocations with *sound*
3 1 great
2 painful
3 boring
4 uncomfortable
5 romantic
6 fascinating

Translation
4 Translate the sentences into your language. Check with your teacher.

6 Reading
1 1 c   2 b   3 d   4 a

2 1 T
2 F (In 2020, 1.6 billion people will go on holiday abroad.)
3 F (Most travellers don't know that planes are bad for the planet.)
4 F (Carbon-neutral travellers want to offset the CO_2 they generate.)
5 T
6 F (If you plant ten trees, it neutralizes the effect of around six tonnes of CO_2.)
7 F (Trees will not take care of the situation.)
8 F (The ultimate answer to the CO_2 problem lies with international organizations.)

3 1 b   2 c   3 e   4 f   5 d   6 a

4 1 b   2 d   3 c   4 a

🔊 Read & listen
5 🔊 24 Refer to Reading 6 *What is the **real** price of tourism?* on page 33.

7a Moving

Present perfect continuous 1
1 1 been doing   2 gone back   3 started
4 travelled   5 been thinking   6 been   7 been

2 1 has been/'s been
2 have done/'ve done
3 have been living/'ve been living
4 have lived/'ve lived
5 have been learning/'ve been learning
6 have been painting/'ve been painting

3 1 since   2 for   3 for   4 since   5 for   6 since

Phrasal verbs with *live*
4 1 out of   2 on   3 through   4 up to   5 for

Dictation
5 🔊 25
A: I've been living out of a suitcase for two months!
B: Well, I hope you've been washing your clothes now and then.
A: Very funny! I've been eating in restaurants for sixty-one days.
B: Terrible!
A: Yeah! Anyway, I'm going.
B: Going to leave the job?
A: No. Going to eat. It's seven and I'm hungry!

🔊 Read & listen
6 🔊 26 Refer to the reading text *Redundancy was the best thing that ever happened to me* on page 66 of the Student's Book.

7B Life changes

Metaphor

1 1 b   2 e   3 a   4 c   5 g   6 d   7 f

2 1 c   2 a   3 b   4 e   5 f   6 d

Vocabulary from the lesson

3 1 c/g/k   2 b   3 d   4 a   5 c/g/k   6 e
7 h   8 f   9 c/g/k   10 i   11 l   12 j

Translation

4 Translate the text into your language. Check with your teacher.

7C Happy birthday

Present perfect continuous 2

1 1 passed   2 remembered   3 been working
4 loved   5 been doing   6 has ever worked

2 1 have decided
2 have experienced/'ve experienced
3 has not been/hasn't been
4 have been seeing/'ve been seeing
5 have been arguing/'ve been arguing
6 have talked/'ve talked/have been talking

3 1 b   2 f   3 a   4 d   5 e   6 c

Life stages

4 1 elderly   2 adolescent   3 thirty something
4 older teenager   5 toddler   6 retired

Dictation

5 🔘 27

I've been retired for about ten months now and I love it.
I've been doing all those things I never had time to do.
I've been working in the garden and I've been painting the house. I've finished the kitchen and bathroom. Retired?
I've never been so busy!

🔘 **Read & listen**

6 🔘 28 Refer to the reading text *Florrie prepares to celebrate her 113th birthday* on page 70 of the Student's Book.

7D Dilemmas

Exclamations with *what*

1 1 b   2 c   3 a   4 b   5 b   6 c

Giving advice

2 1 You have to speak   2 If I were you,
3 There's no harm in   4 Tell him you
5 What you need to do

Translation

3 Translate the advert into your language. Check with your teacher.

7 Reading

1 1 e   2 a   3 d   4 b   5 c

2 1 d   2 a   3 b   4 c

---

3 1 They have been working harder and for longer hours.
2 To spend more time with the family.
3 Financial problems, a lack of mental stimulation, a feeling that they are no longer valued in society.
4 94% say that they are happy with their choice and only 6% say that they are unhappy.

🔘 **Read & listen**

4 🔘 29 Refer to Reading 7 *Downshifting – a way of living* on page 38.

8A Breaking news

Newspapers

1 1 h   2 e   3 f   4 c   5 b   6 a   7 d   8 g

Would

2 1 hate   2 mind   3 never   4 'd   5 like
6 wouldn't   7 to be

3 1 c   2 e   3 a   4 b   5 f   6 d

Translation

4 Translate the text into your language. Check with your teacher.

8B Protests

Unreal conditions (type 2)

1 1 a   2 c   3 f   4 b   5 e   6 d

2 2 three million fewer people would die every year
3 save up to 10% off their heating bills if they turned down the heating by 1°C in winter
4 If they ate well or exercised enough

3 What would that be like; our life would collapse; It would be like a terrible dream; It wouldn't be a happy world; If such a thing happened; I wouldn't want to live in such a world

Dictation

4 🔘 30

How would you feel if you didn't earn enough money?
What would you do? Would you go on strike? Would you demonstrate in the street? Remember action is better than inaction, so if I were you, I'd get going!

8C Bank robbers

Unreal conditions (type 3)

1 1 If the bag hadn't split open, they wouldn't have lost any money.
2 If the accident hadn't happened on a busy motorway, they wouldn't have lost so much money.
3 If some people hadn't stopped to help them, they would have rescued even less money.
4 They would have been £10,500 richer if they had taken a cheque instead of cash.
5 The police would never have been suspicious if they hadn't had so much money in cash on them.
6 If they had travelled by train, they wouldn't have lost a penny.

2 2 evidence, he wouldn't have been arrested by the police
3 the burglar if he hadn't called his mother from his victim's house

Law & order
3 1 robber   2 evidence   3 arrested   4 robbery
5 trial   6 judge   7 guilty   8 sentenced

🔊 Read & listen
4 🔊 **31** Refer to the reading text on page 81 of the Student's Book.

8D Driving
Offers
1 1 Can I do something for you?
2 I'll give you a hand if you like.
3 Let me help you
4 What would you like me to do?
5 Do you want me to type it up for you?
6 Shall I start now?

2 1 c   2 a   3 b   4 a   5 c

Compound nouns (driving)
3 1 driving licence   2 one-way street   3 speed limit
4 motorway   5 traffic light   6 no-parking zone

Dictation
4 🔊 **32**
1 **A:** Excuse me, sir. I wouldn't park there if I were you. It's a no-parking zone.
B: Oh, thank you.
2 **C:** Can I give you a hand with that?
D: No, thanks. I'll manage.
3 **E:** Would you like me to check your homework?
F: Yes, that's really kind of you.
4 **G:** Would you mind showing me your driving licence?
H: No, not at all. Here you are.

8 Reading
1 a 3   b 1   c 4   d 2
2 **Paragraph 1:** Newspaper sales aren't rising all over the world. (they are falling in Europe)
Paragraph 2: … they have made money through advertising although people aren't prepared to pay to read them.
Paragraph 3: … they're available twenty-four hours a day.
Paragraph 4: In the future, the news will arrive as it happens.

3 1 revenue   2 broadsheets   3 real-time news
4 thriving   5 up-to-the-minute news

🔊 Read & listen
4 🔊 **33** Refer to Reading 8 *The future of the press?* on page 43.

9A The shopping basket
Articles & determiners
1 1 a   2 the   3 the   4 some   5 some
6 any   7 the   8 the

2 1 The   2 –   3 Some   4 any/–   5 a
6 –   7 –   8 any

Containers
3 1 ice cream, margarine
2 coffee, strawberry jam
3 beer, whisky, milk, mineral water, olive oil
4 biscuits, crackers, crisps, peanuts, tissues, coffee
5 tomato soup, dog food, tuna
6 tissues
7 beer, tomato soup, dog food, tuna
8 tomato soup, free-range eggs, milk

4 1 jar/packet   2 packet   3 tin   4 carton   5 bottle
6 carton   7 tub

Dictation
5 🔊 **34**
A: Perfect Pizza. Good evening.
B: Oh, hi. I'd like to order some pizza, please? Cheese and tomato?
A: OK. A small, medium or large one?
B: Large.
A: And would you like any toppings?
B: Err, yes … some tuna and black olives, please.
A: Oh, I'm sorry, but we don't have any black ones. Green OK?
B: That's fine.
A: OK, that's a large cheese and tomato pizza with tuna and green olives.

🔊 Read & listen
6 🔊 **35** Refer to the reading text *Checking out the check out* on page 87 of the Student's Book.

9B Shoppers
Quantifiers 1
1 1 most   2 Many   3 most   4 most
5 all   6 most   7 none   8 any

Shopping
2 1 shopping centre/mall   2 shop assistant
3 security guard   4 shoplifters   5 window shopping
6 high street shopping   7 shopaholic   8 online shopping

Translation
3 Translate the sentences into your language. Check with your teacher.

9C E-shopping
Collocations with *take*
1 1 a little time   2 breath away   3 a look at
4 advantage of   5 our word   6 advice

Quantifiers 2
2 1 many   2 plenty   3 A lot of   4 little
5 a few   6 little   7 a few

3 Netaholic answers: 1 e   2 e   3 a   4 a   5 a   6 e

Dictation

4 💿 36

Too much to do and not enough time to do it? Take my advice and shop online. There are plenty of good reasons. Shop when and where you want. And remember that spending a little time can actually save you loads of time and money. The choice is never-ending, whether you're buying a few Christmas presents or buying a new dishwasher. So why wait?

9D Phone calls

Complaints

1 1 I think there's something wrong with this laptop.
2 Well, I only bought it yesterday and I'm having problems with the speakers.
3 No, they just don't work.
4 But I want to have my money back.
5 I'm sorry, but this is unacceptable.
6 Could I speak to the manager, please?

Vocabulary from the lesson

2 1 b   2 a/h   3 d   4 c   5 f   6 g   7 a/h   8 e

Prepositional phrases

3 1 in   2 in   3 in   4 in   5 On   6 by   7 in   8 by

4 1 b   2 e   3 g   4 c   5 f   6 d   7 a   8 h

Translation

5 Translate the dialogue into your language. Check with your teacher.

9 Reading

1 a 3   b 1   c 2

2 1 a   2 b   3 b   4 a   5 b   6 a

3 1 internationally renowned   2 huge
3 bewildering array   4 scorching   5 essential
6 opulent   7 boom   8 transformed   9 sheer

💿 Read & listen

4 💿 37 Refer to Reading 9 *The world's greatest shopping malls* on page 48.

10A Secrets

Modals of speculation 1 (present time)

1 2 She can't be French.
3 She could be divorced.
4 She might have children.
5 She may smoke.
6 She might play the piano.
7 She must live in Birmingham.

Illusions

2 1 magician   2 perform   3 Audiences   4 tricks
5 vanish   6 pretending   7 fake   8 magical

Dictation

3 💿 38

A: It's obviously a woman's handbag.
B: Yeah. And I think she must be Costa Rican.
A: Well, she could be French, you know.
B: Why would she have a cassette for learning French? She can't be French.
A: OK, OK. She might study French.
B: Uh-huh. And she may be married …
A: Or divorced?
B: Yeah. Oh, and I think she lives in Birmingham.
A: Yes, there's a mobile phone bill with an address in Birmingham on it. She lives there.

10B Fact or fiction?

Word families

1 1 likelihood   2 probability   3 impossible   4 certainty
5 possibility

2 1 likelihood   2 improbable   3 definitely
4 impossible   5 uncertain   6 probably
7 possibility   8 certainly   9 probability   10 unlikely

Modals of speculation 2 (present time)

3 1 b   2 a   3 c   4 b

Translation

4 Translate the text into your language. Check with your teacher.

10C Mysteries

Modals of speculation (past time)

1 1 must have been drawn
2 could the Nazca people have managed
3 must have been
4 could they have been used
5 might have been
6 could have had

Verbs followed by infinitive

2 1 claimed to   2 tried to   3 deserved to
4 seemed to   5 began to   6 managed to

Dictation

3 💿 39

A: Well, this is a mystery. Where could I have put my car keys?
B: Have you tried to look in your jacket pockets?
A: Don't be silly! Ah, but I might have left them in the office.
B: No, you can't have done. How would you have got home without your car keys?
A: Good point. Well, how about the kitchen? I might have left them there.
B: Oh, look. Here they are.
A: Thanks, darling. Now where have I put my glasses?

10D Strictly confidential

Advantages & disadvantages

1 1 N   2 P   3 N   4 P   5 P   6 N   7 N   8 N

2 1 testing   2 benefits   3 disadvantage
4 trouble   5 problem   6 advantage

Idioms

3 1 cracking   2 high point   3 to the point
4 it safe   5 dragging your feet   6 bright and early

Translation

4 Translate the dialogue into your own language. Check with your teacher.

10 Reading

1 1 c   2 c   3 c   4 b   5 c

2 Lord Lucan vanished *one* day after his *nanny* was horribly murdered; New DNA techniques *could* help police to solve the case; he was *found guilty* of the murder; by meeting him in France and driving him to *another* country; he was an *ex-schoolteacher*

📀 Read & listen

3 📀 **40** Refer to Reading 10 *'Lucky' Lord Lucan – alive or dead?* on page 53.

11A Total sport

Passive

1 1 was born   2 was being practised
3 was always being attacked   4 could be
5 were founded   6 were opened
7 is not allowed   8 was established

2 1 was written   2 was practised   3 was included
4 were covered   5 was revived   6 has been practised
7 is also promoted   8 were cut   9 was pulled
10 was needed   11 was developed   12 has been
13 are flying

Sport 1: boxing   **Sport 2:** paragliding

Sport

3 1 athletics   2 baseball   3 boxing
4 rugby   5 water polo

Dictation

4 📀 **41**
As you know, the Olympics are held every four years. The 2004 games were held in Athens and watched by over four billion people, and in 2008, they took place in Beijing. The Olympic village for the next Olympics is being built as I speak and will house thousands of athletes and officials. Hopefully, it's going to be finished in time.

11B Olympic dreams

Nouns & adjectives (describing people)

1 1 agile   2 intelligence   3 ruthlessness
4 enthusiastically   5 determined   6 ambition
7 talented   8 power

Verbs with two objects

2 2 The Queen gave the winning team the trophy.
3 The Greeks built the athletes a massive Olympic village.
4 The athlete won her country a gold medal.
5 The winner gave the journalists a press conference.

Translation

3 Translate the sentences into your own language. Check with your teacher.

11C Strange sports

Causative

1 1 He has his shirt, shorts and boots made for him (by a major company).
2 She has (her) dresses designed for her (by a top fashion house).
3 He has his bat and his cap sponsored (by a major drinks company).
4 He has ten new racquets delivered to his house every week (by his sponsors).
5 He has his boots cleaned for him every time he plays in a match (by an apprentice player).
6 They have their bats checked after each inning to make sure they are in perfect condition (by an expert).

2 a 2, 4   b 3, 6   c 1, 5

Services

3 1 served   2 cooked   3 delivered   4 designed
5 ironed   6 cut   7 serviced   8 tested

Dictation

4 📀 **42**
Welcome to *Guess the sporting personality*. Here are your three clues. Number one: he had photos taken with a famous actress for *Hi* magazine and his wife was furious. Two: his club has had a new contract written up, but he won't sign it. And number three: he's just had his hair cut for a new advertising campaign, but his sponsors don't like it. So who is he?

11D Sport relief

Make & do

1 1 to make   2 to do   3 made   4 to do   5 make
6 to do   7 do   8 do

Question tags (checking)

2 1 aren't you   2 can't you   3 haven't you
4 could we   5 won't you   6 are you
7 won't you

3 1 isn't it   2 haven't you   3 doesn't it
4 could you   5 aren't you   6 couldn't you

Translation

4 Translate the advert into your language. Check with your teacher.

11 Reading

1 1 T   2 F (The race takes place in the countryside near Llanwrtyd Wells.)   3 T   4 F (The first cyclist to beat a horse was Tim Gould in 1989.)   5 T   6 F (Huw Lobb managed to beat a horse in the race in 2004.)

2 1 It was invented in Scotland (on the coast).
2 It takes place each June.
3 It took place in 1980.
4 Welsh runner Guto Nyth Bran may have inspired him.
5 The challenge of trying to beat a horse and the prize money on offer.
6 He ran well in the London Marathon.

3 1 obsessed   2 bizarre   3 demanding   4 overheard
5 attract   6 inevitable   7 tough

Read & listen

4 **43** Refer to Reading 11 *Britain's most unusual sporting event* on page 58.

12A Basic needs

Reported speech & thought

1 2 She told Richard that his father had left him four million pounds and two sports cars.
3 Richard said that he didn't know what to say but he was going to drink to his father that night.
4 He told the solicitor he hadn't spoken to his father for ten years.
5 He said that he could finally pay off his debts.
6 He told the solicitor he would give the rest of the money to a homeless charity.
7 The solicitor said that his father had also given him a house with fourteen bedrooms.

2 2 'Your father has left you four million pounds and two sports cars.'
3 'I don't know what to say, but I'm going to drink to my father this evening.'
4 'I haven't spoken to my father for ten years.'
5 'I can finally pay off my debts.'
6 'I'll give the rest of the money to a homeless charity.'
7 'Your father has also given you a house with fourteen bedrooms.'

3 1 She told me that …
2 He said he wanted a steady job …
3 He told me that the most important …
4 She told me that …
5 … her daughter was ill …
6 He said that he wanted a roof …

Vocabulary from the lesson

4 1 to fly home   2 your time   3 fall in love
4 homeless   5 a mortgage   6 between hours

Dictation

5 **44**
In a 1997 British survey, people were given a list of ten things. They had to say which of these things were important for making them happy. 59% of people said that being healthy was the most important thing, followed by family life at 41%. When asked if money brought happiness, 25% of people said having money didn't make them happy, but not having it would make them unhappy.

12B Money

Reported questions

1 1 saw   2 were still seeing   3 you lived   4 would
5 were   6 had been married   7 would do

Vocabulary from the lesson

2 1 d   2 c   3 b   4 a   5 f   6 h   7 e   8 g

Translation

3 Translate the text into your own language. Check with your teacher.

12C Sue!

Tell & ask with infinitive

1 1 her   2 not to   3 not to   4 to stop   5 asked
6 to call   7 her to   8 Eva

2 1 asked the plaintiff to explain   2 told the company to pay
3 asked the court not to   4 told her lawyer to sue
5 her client not to   6 asked the plaintiff to speak

Reporting verbs

3 1 d   2 f   3 b   4 c   5 e   6 a

4 1 denied   2 informed   3 complained
4 insisted   5 warned

12D Golden moments

Social expressions

1 1 b   2 b   3 c   4 c   5 b
2 1 g   2 e   3 a   4 b   5 f   6 c   7 d

Vocabulary from the lesson

3 1 c   2 a/f   3 d/g   4 b   5 h   6 e   7 d/g   8 a/f

Dictation

4 **45**
If you're listening to this, you've made it to the end of the workbook. That's excellent news. Congratulations! It's not easy learning another language, but you've come a long way. Take care and good luck with your English!

12 Reading

1 1 c   2 b   3 c   4 c   5 b   6 a

2 1 c   2 a   3 a   4 b   5 c

Read & listen

3 **46** Refer to Reading 12 on page 63.

Writing answer key

1 A description of a best friend
Reading
1 1 d   2 c   3 a   4 b

2 1 much bigger than me   2 a bit impatient
3 looks like his father

Language focus
1 a 2   b 3   c 7   d 6   e 4   f 1   g 5

3 Physically, he is average build and quite tall. He has got a pale complexion and blond curly hair, but the first thing you notice about him is his moustache. I wouldn't describe him as good-looking, but he has an interesting face. He has lively blue eyes and a prominent nose that lots of women seem to like.

4 *Sample answer:*
Dave is short and has fair hair, although he is going a little bald. He wears old-fashioned clothes and has small round glasses. He's muscular and very fit and although he's in his forties, he still thinks he's good-looking!

Writing
3 *Sample answer:*
My best friend is Lucy. The first time I met her was when we were at university together. At first I thought she was rather boring and also a bit arrogant, but later on I got to know her and found out that she was really good company. She's an excellent listener and can be really good fun. Unfortunately, we don't see each other very often as she lives in another city. Many people say that Lucy is very difficult to get to know. She gives the impression of being rather self-centred, but that really isn't true. She actually has a wonderful sense of humour and is very down-to-earth once you get to know her. Physically she is really beautiful. She is tall and slim and has got really long legs. She has got a tanned complexion, long curly black hair and a lovely smile. The first thing you notice about her are her eyes – they are a deep brown and sparkle when she smiles. She's into lots of things, especially music, but she hates nightclubs! She's really good at dancing. She loves salsa and she belongs to a dancing club. She's quite keen on going out to concerts, watching films and spending time with her friends and family.

2 A description of a town or city
Reading
1 2
2 1 c   2 a   3 d   4 b

3 Answers with ticks: 1, 3, 4, 5, 7, 9.

Language focus
2 excellent museums; wonderful food; unbelievable nightlife; outstanding live music scene; exceptional museums; superb collections; marvellous weather; impressive Plaza Mayor; spectacular Prado museum; first-rate collection of European art

5 If you're in Brussels in April or May, don't miss a visit to the Royal Palace at Laeken with its beautiful gardens and greenhouses. The greenhouses were built for King Leopold II of Belgium, who was also responsible for the nearby Japanese tower, which sometimes houses temporary exhibitions.

Writing
1 *Sample answer:*
Budapest is the capital of Hungary and is the perfect destination for a short weekend break or a longer holiday. Visitors are attracted by the city's history, its historical buildings, its great architecture and the excellent museums as well as its fabulous hospitality. The people are some of the friendliest you will meet and the excellent food and wine makes Budapest one of the most popular places to visit in Europe. Originally Budapest was two towns – Buda and Pest – one on either side of the river Danube. In 1873, the two towns were joined to create Budapest. There are many places of interest in the city, but a must for all visitors is Castle Hill with its cobbled streets, castle walls and Matthias Church. From here you get an amazing panoramic view of the whole city. Another place well worth visiting is Heroes Square with its monument and the big park – Városliget with a small lake and the city zoo. When the weather is good why not take a day trip up the river Danube to the small town of Szentendre? This picturesque town is full of artists and small museums and makes an ideal break from the city. In the evening enjoy a walk down one of the city streets or along the banks of the Danube. You might want to go to the top of Gellért Hill and see the city lights at night. For those of you interested in culture you can go to the theatre or enjoy some wonderful opera at really reasonable prices. Finally, why not visit a traditional 'wine house' where you can drink delicious Hungarian wine or go to one of the many restaurants? People here enjoy life and Budapest has something for everyone.

3 Advantages and disadvantages
Reading
1 3

2 1 for: life is usually cheaper (food and accommodation are usually subsidized); you don't have to deal with things that go wrong in rented accommodation; you save time by being close to the library (so you have more time to study)
2 against: you can lose contact with the real world; you don't have as much independence or freedom; it isn't necessary to develop the same life skills as you do living off campus

Language focus
1 **making your first point:** For a start; First of all
making additional points: Secondly; What is more
making your last point: Finally

2 *Sample answer:*
There are many good reasons for studying a foreign language in the country of the language. For a start, you are surrounded by the language and can learn a lot without really making any effort. Moreover, there are many opportunities to learn about the culture, and this can be extremely interesting. Finally, the progress that you make will probably be much faster.

3 1 normally 2 believe; accommodation
3 usually; necessary 4 independence; responsibilities
5 recommend 6 managing

Writing

1 1 A 2 D 3 A 4 D 5 D
6 A 7 A 8 A 9 D 10 D

3 *Sample answer:*
There are a lot of advantages to studying abroad. Firstly, it's a great opportunity to meet different kinds of people and make new friends. You will often meet people from all around the world. Moreover, it allows you to learn about a new culture and experience things that you wouldn't if you stayed in your own country. Learning about different cultures and meeting new people can only be a positive thing. On top of this, it looks really good on your CV and future employers are likely to be impressed.
However, there are some disadvantages, too. First of all, it can be quite hard to adapt to different food and customs and this can cause problems. What is more, you don't have the support from friends and family and so, if anything goes wrong, you are on your own. Finally, as there are so many new and interesting things, it can be difficult to study with so many distractions. To sum up, although there are as many pros as cons, I believe that overall the advantages for studying abroad are stronger than the disadvantages. As a result, I would recommend people study abroad if they have the chance.

4 A narrative: lottery winner

Reading

1 1 b 2 c 3 a

2 Correct order: 7, 6, 4, 5, 1, 2, 3

3 1 d 2 a 3 e 4 b 5 c

Language focus

2 1 At first 2 First of all 3 finally 4 eventually

3 the Belfast woman; the mother-of-two; the lucky winner; 58-year-old Iris; the UK's latest winner; the grandmother-to-be; Mrs Jeffrey

4 *Sample answer:*
The 42-year-old had spent it all; the unlucky gambler soon ran out of money; Mr Pratt sold his car; the Dublin man told reporters

5 1 'And the final winning number is 49,' said the man on the radio.
2 'I thought I'd give it a go, but I never thought I'd win,' he said.
3 'I used my parents' birthdays to choose the numbers,' he explained.
4 He turned round to his passenger and said, 'I've just won the lottery.'
5 'You're kidding,' he said.
6 'The most incredible thing happened to me today,' he told his wife.

Writing

2 *Sample answer:*
'I couldn't believe it,' said John Townsend when asked about his lottery win. John, a taxi driver from Glasgow in Scotland, had never played the lottery before. 24-year-old John became Britain's youngest lottery winner when he won the £15 million jackpot. He had used his mother and father's birthdays to pick the numbers. Mr Townsend was driving his taxi when he heard the winning numbers on the radio. 'I was so shocked, I just had to stop,' he said. He was driving a passenger at the time. 'I told him he'd have to take another cab,' explained John. 'Of course, he wasn't very happy, but after a while I just wanted to phone my wife and tell her what had happened.' With his winnings, Britain's youngest winner says he wants to take care of his family. 'The first thing I'm going to do is buy my parents a new house,' John told reporters. He also plans to buy a bigger house for his family, wife Joan and their two young children. Finally, after going on holiday, John plans to start his own taxi company.

5 An advertisement

Reading

1 1 d 2 b 3 e 4 a 5 c

2 Direct flights to four top destinations – W; Ten flights a day – W; Journey time 4 hours 10 minutes – M; Basic fare £180 – M; Free travel insurance – W; Book early and get 5% off – M; Sandwiches and snacks on board – M

Language focus

1 1 reliable 2 efficient 3 unbeatable 4 stylish
5 memorable 6 delicious 7 incredible
8 unbelievable

2 1, 5 and 6 are not full sentences.

3 1 There are/We offer two departures a day, seven days a week, 52 weeks a year.
2 Are you looking for low fares & quality service?
3 We offer/There are last minute offers.
4 We offer all of this at discount rates./All of this is at discount rates.
5 Delicious meals are prepared by top-class chefs.
6 There is/We offer an incredible choice of ten music channels and the very latest movies.
7 Are you travelling to Moscow or St Petersburg?

4 1 at 2 before 3 Like 4 to 5 on 6 only
7 for 8 With

Writing

1 London Victoria to six top destinations; Poznan and Wroclaw; help you with hotel bookings; connections to more than; With a journey time; between London and Warsaw; there is no better

3 *Sample answer:*
And like any good travel operator, we also offer a variety of additional services including hotel bookings and travel insurance to help make your stay in Poland as pleasant as possible. With MillanTours you will travel in style. All our coaches are non-smoking and have air conditioning and toilet and washroom facilities. Naturally, all our coaches have easy access for disabled passengers and the onboard telephone means you can stay in touch with friends and family back home.

During your journey we will try and make you as comfortable as possible. Light snacks and hot and cold drinks are served on all our trips. In addition, we show some of the latest films and other programmes on our onboard video and the panoramic windows give you the opportunity to see some of the most beautiful countryside as we drive through Europe. With the lowest prices around we offer you unbeatable choice at unbeatable value. One-way tickets are £60 and a return is £100. Buy your tickets using our easy internet booking system and save 5%. There are no extra charges and a money back guarantee for any journeys with a delay of more than five hours. Where else can you get a deal like that? You can rely on us to make this a memorable experience for you. So, book now and you'll be in Poland before you know it.

6 An extract from a holiday brochure

Reading
1 1 b   2 c   3 a

2 1 b   2 e   3 c   4 a   5 f   6 d

3 1 c   2 e   3 b   4 d   5 g   6 f   7 a

Language focus
1 1 it's   2 it's 3   island's   4 Caribbean's   5 islanders'

2 Our exclusive hotel, *The Coconut Club*, is situated near Marigot Bay, on the west coast, only a short drive from Castries. Set in 70 acres of palm trees; a short walk to the bars; Located between Martinique and St Vincent

4 1 like   2 for example   3 including

Writing
1 *Sample answer:*
Our exclusive hotel, the *Maui Sunrise*, is situated on the west coast of the island close to the beach. The four-star hotel has breathtaking views of the ocean and excellent facilities. The hotel has its own golf course, as well as a tennis centre and a swimming pool. There are two superb restaurants, one of which serves traditional local dishes while the other has a selection of international food. In the evening enjoy a drink in one of our two bars before dancing the night away in our exclusive nightclub. The *Maui Sunrise* is relaxed but elegant and certainly the place to stay when you visit the island.
When you feel like a day away from the beach, it's easy to find activities for all the family. Take your pick from our huge range of excursions. Visit Haleakala National Park, home of the biggest dormant volcano in the world. Alternatively, you could go whale-watching, take a helicopter tour of the island or simply walk around the streets of the old capital Lahaina. If you're looking for an action-packed holiday, why not go mountain biking down the volcano at sunrise? There is also a wide range of water sports such as kayaking, sailing and surfing. Located in the middle of the Pacific Ocean, the volcanic island of Maui is the biggest island in the Hawaiian chain. With its stunning long sandy beaches, its tropical forests and the cosmopolitan resorts of Kapalua and Makena, Maui is a tropical paradise and has everything you could ever want, making it the perfect holiday destination.

7 A letter of advice

Reading
1 3

Language focus
1 1 You could start by getting
2 You could always get
3 Why not try
4 the best thing you can do
5 the first thing I would do is see
6 what about finding out

2 2 I think it might be a good idea to take out a student loan.
3 Why don't you talk to your parents?/Why not talk to your parents?
4 The first thing I would do/you should do/to do is find a part-time job.
5 Why not speak to a financial advisor?
6 You could start by asking about scholarships.

3 1 I can sympathize with your situation.
2 I know it all seems very difficult.
3 I wish you luck.
4 Don't give up!
5 All the best.
6 I'm sure everything will work out fine.

4 a 4, 6;   b 3, 5;   c 1, 2

Writing
1 1 B   2 A   3 B   4 A
3 *Sample answer:*
Dear Sarah,
I think it's great that you've started your own business and that things are going so well and I understand that it must be difficult to balance everything when you have two young children. The first thing I would do would be to try and find an assistant who can help you with your business. I'm sure there are lots of people who would love to work with you. However, if this isn't possible then I'd think about putting your business on hold until your children are older. Remember, your children will only be young once and you really don't want to miss out on this special time. I think you might find that as your children grow up you will have more time and you won't have to wait too long, you may even find that your children want to help you making the jewellery. Finally, whatever you decide, discuss it with your husband and make sure he understands your decision, it will make it easier for him to give you any support you need.
Good luck!
Danni

8 A funny crime story

Reading
1 4

2 Correct order: 3, 2, 1, 4, 8, 7, 6, 5

Language focus
2 1 therefore   2 so   3 because   4 therefore
5 Consequently   6 As a result of

3 1 the stolen car   2 Sandy Jason
   3 Bill Madison and Sandy Jason   4 the camera
   5 Bill Madison   6 the car

4 she was chatting; she saw; he couldn't get; She went over to help him but it was too heavy; Together, they helped the man; When they were all; She thought that; and she therefore decided to watch him

Writing

1 Correct order: d, b, a, c

2 *Sample answer:*
She watched the man carefully as he wheeled himself down one of the aisles. The man seemed to be spending as much time watching her as he was looking at the books. Angie watched in disbelief as the man began to take books from the shelves and put them under the blanket that covered his knees. Still not quite believing what she was seeing, Angie went over to talk to the store detective. He had also noticed the man taking books from the shelf and hiding them, so they decided to go and talk to the young man and ask him if he was going to pay for the books. However, the man had seen the two of them talking to each other and so, as they approached him, he jumped out of the wheelchair and ran towards the door. 'I couldn't believe it,' Angie said, 'one minute he was sitting in his wheelchair and the next minute he was running straight out of the shop.' Because of his hurry to leave, he failed to notice a woman in a wheelchair just outside the shop door. As a result, the man fell over her and landed heavily on the pavement. Consequently, Angie and the store detective caught the man and he was arrested.

9 A letter of complaint

Reading

1 c

Language focus

1 1 c   2 d   3 b   4 a

2 a 2   b 3   c 1   d 3

3 b 5   c 2   d 4   e 11   f 3
   g 1   h 10   i 9   j 7   k 8

5 2, 3 and 6 are grammatically incorrect.

6 1 Although they guarantee same-day delivery, the flowers arrived three days late.
   2 The flowers finally arrived. However, they were sent to the wrong address./They were sent to the wrong address, however.
   3 Mum was very disappointed, although she saw the funny side of it. Although Mum was very disappointed, she saw the funny side of it.
   4 I had never used the company before. However, friends had told me that they were very good./Friends had told me that they were very good, however.

Writing

1 3

3 *Sample answer:*
Dear Sir/Madam,
I am writing to complain about your online delivery service which I used to deliver some flowers to my mother for Mother's Day. I ordered a bouquet of roses to be delivered to my mother using your online service. I had never used your company before. However, friends had told me you were pretty good. Although your website guarantees same-day delivery, the flowers arrived three days late. To make matters worse, when they finally arrived they were delivered to the wrong address.
I am afraid that I find this situation totally unacceptable and would like a full and immediate refund. The order number is MD1057/3. If I do not hear from you within the next week, I shall take legal advice. Please contact me by email or by phone on 01865 960811.
I look forward to hearing from you and to a quick resolution of this problem.
Yours faithfully,

10 A narrative

Reading

1 Correct order: 2, 3, 4, 1

Language focus

1 absolutely; mysterious; disappearance; worried; eventually; customer; received; lawyer; discovering; vanished

2 1 That   2 Before   3 within   4 Later   5 after   6 at

4 1 Thinking about his plans to buy a new house, he was in a good mood.
   2 Feeling frightened, he called his lawyer.
   3 Closing the shop, he went to see his lawyer.
   4 Sitting down in the chair, the customer asked Templar about the posters on the walls.
   5 Discovering the man's name, the family knew they were close to the truth.
   6 Knowing they were in trouble, the Sheards decided to disappear.

Writing

1 1 d   2 b   3 a   4 c   5 e
2 *Sample answer:*
On a hot day in June, the Wilson family were getting ready to go on holiday. Although they were late and they had a plane to catch, Mrs Wilson was still giving last minute instructions to Monica, who was looking after the house while they were away on holiday. Seeing the taxi arrive, Mrs Wilson gave one final instruction before hurrying out of the house. Monica was happy thinking about the week she would spend in the large, beautiful house with its lovely big garden. She wandered into the kitchen and saw a note stuck to the fridge door. It read, 'Food in freezer, help yourself.' Smiling, she opened the fridge and made herself a sandwich.
Later that afternoon, Monica went out into the garden. It was a beautiful day, the sun was shining and Monica felt a bit hot. Looking at the cool swimming pool, she started dreaming about how nice it would be to go for a quick swim. After changing into her swimming costume, she ran out into the garden and dived into the pool. A minute later she was sitting at the edge of the pool looking at the dead fish floating on the surface.

Panicking, she realized she must have killed it! What should she do?

The next day Monica went out to find a shop that sold fish. Walking along the high street, she found one and was happy when she found that they sold the same type of fish as the dead one in the swimming pool. Hoping the family wouldn't notice that the fish was new, she bought it and took it back to the Wilsons'. The following week, the Wilson family came home. They had had a really good holiday and were all happy and suntanned. After saying goodbye to Monica, and thanking her for looking after the house, they all went out into the garden. Walking over to the swimming pool, Mrs Wilson was so horrified to see a fish swimming around that she screamed!

11 A description of a sporting event

Reading

1 1 b   2 a   3 d   4 c

2 Sentences with ticks: 2, 4, 6, 7, 8

Language focus

2 1 so that   2 in order to
3 so as to   4 in order that

4 1 d   2 b   3 a   4 c

5 greatest marathons, attracting more than 85,000 applicants; $500,000, but many; 2,000,000 spectators; marathons, the runners; fund raisers, fun runners and amateurs; Mark P says, 'Crossing the finish line

6 1 f   2 d   3 a   4 c   5 e   6 b

Writing

2 *Sample answer:*
The Iditarod Trail Sled Dog Race in Alaska is one of the most famous in the world. It was started almost 90 years ago when people needed to get to the town of Nome for medicine, but the first international race was held in 1972. In 2005, there were competitors from over 30 countries. The annual event takes place in March in Anchorage, Alaska and is over 1,100 miles long. It finishes in Nome on the north-west coast. Competitors leave Anchorage on sleds pulled by Huskies (big dogs that are used to pulling sledges over snow) in order to race across some of the hardest terrain possible. Temperatures often fall to around –50°, making it one of the most difficult races in the world. The current record is eight days, twenty-two hours. The race receives lots of applications and the deadline for entries is December 1. All competitors must be qualified 'mushers' (people who race sleds and Huskies). Full details are available on the official website, so that spectators can get information about the race route and event.
Anyone who has seen the race will tell you that it is an incredible sight. Every year hundreds of spectators travel to the towns along the route so as to see the sleds entering and leaving the towns. In recent years, the number of spectators has increased as the fame of the race has spread around the world.

12 Writing a report

Reading

1 1 £59   2 £6.20   3 30   4 70

2 1 T
2 F (The report looks at how much an average family spends, what they spend it on and how spending changes with age.)
3 F (People generally spend more on sport and other free time activities than food and drink.)
4 T
5 T
6 F (Older people generally spend more on food and drink than younger people.)

Language focus

1 a 8   b 3, 4   c 7   d 1   e 2   f 3, 4   g 6   h 5

2 1 The average British family spends £453 a week.
2 They spend more on transport than anything else.
3 Health and education come at the bottom of the list.
4 People aged 30 to 45 spend the most.
5 The amount of money people spend on food increases with age.

Writing

1 1 10,000   2 between May 2005 and January 2006
3 £13.00   4 girls   5 girls 12–16   6 boys 12–16
7 boys 7–11   8 girls – clothes & shoes; boys – other food

3 *Sample answer:*
10,000 children took part in this year's survey. The data was collected over a period of ten months from May 2005 to January 2006. This report represents the main results of this survey into children's spending habits.

General summary
The survey shows that the average child spends £13.00 a week. They spend more on sweets and snacks than on anything else, with an average of £2.50 per week. Other food purchases come next with an average of £2.40 spent on this category. This is followed by clothes and shoes, with £2.00 being spent and then games, music and DVDs, with an average of £1.60 spent on these items. Finally, toys, hobbies and pets come bottom of the list, with only £1.20 spent on these items.

Breakdown of specific information
The results also show how spending varies with age and by gender. There is little significant difference in the spending habits of boys and girls on sweets, snacks and food items, with only a 20 pence difference. However, girls spend almost three times as much on clothes with an average of £2.90 per week, compared to £1.10 spent by boys. The same is not true when it comes to games, music and DVDs, with girls spending only £0.90 per week in comparison to £2.20 by boys. The biggest difference is on spending on toys, hobbies and pets with boys spending up to five times as much as girls with an average of £2.00 per week. There are also significant differences depending on age. The total expenditure for boys and girls of seven to eleven is an average of £7.00 compared to almost £21.00 for those aged twelve to sixteen. Both age groups spend almost 30 per cent on sweets and snacks whereas the proportion of money spent on games, toys, hobbies and pets decreases significantly as children get older.

Conclusion
Overall the amount of money children spend increases as they get older. The items they buy vary with age and with gender. Generally younger children spend more on games, toys, hobbies and pets than older children, and boys spend more than girls on these items.